Jerry Johnston and his wife, Chris, share a lighter moment with an audience.

Jerry's addresses to various communities fill civic arenas like this one.

Jerry answers questions from the news media. Suicide is America's second greatest teenage killer.

Jerry's Life Expose message has been heard by over 2.5 million youth in the U.S.

Aaron Stoufer, fifteen-year-old son of Dennis and Barbara Stoufer, killed himself with a .22 Magnum. (Used courtesy of the *Kansas City Star*.)

WHY SUICIDE?

This special paperback edition of *Why Suicide?* has been designed and imprinted to be given free to teenagers everywhere to help answer the troubling questions about suicide and other problems.

My deepest thanks go to our contributors nationwide who have given financially so that any teenager who wants a copy might obtain one at no cost.

If after reading this important book you feel led to donate in order that this gift might go on, you may use the envelope that has been provided. All gifts are tax deductible. If the envelope is missing, you may send your contribution to the address printed below.

My deepest desire is that millions of lives will be touched before it is too late. Please help me fulfill this dream.

Yours for youth,

Jerry Johnston

Jerry Johnston

Jerry Johnston Association
P.O. Box 12193
Overland Park, Kansas 66212
For personal attention call: (913) 492-2066

Why Suicide?

JERRY JOHNSTON

A Division of Thomas Nelson Publishers
Nashville • Atlanta • Camden • New York

Published in Nashville, Tennessee, by Oliver-Nelson Books, a division of Thomas Nelson, Inc., Publishers, and distributed in Canada by Lawson Falle, Ltd., Cambridge, Ontario.

The excerpt on page 123 is from the Oregon City ENTER-PRISE-COURIER and is reprinted with permission.

The excerpt on page 168 is from an article by Pamela Cantor. Copyright, 1986 USA TODAY. Reprinted with permission.

The photo of Dennis and Barbara Stoufer is used courtesy of the KANSAS CITY STAR.

Unless specifically identified as factual, all names and events have been fictionalized for protection of privacy.

Printed in the United States of America.

Library of Congress Cataloging-in-Publication Data

Johnston, Jerry, 1959–
    Why suicide?

    Bibliography: p.
    1. Youth—United States—Suicidal behavior.
2. Suicide—United States.   I. Title.
HV6546.J65   1987   362.2   86-31165

1 2 3 4 5 6—92 91 90 89 88 87

*To Susan, a promising tenth grader,
who was at home committing suicide
while I was speaking to her classmates
at Bishop Kenny High School
in Jacksonville, Florida.
The memory of Susan and her grieving
friends continues to motivate me
to reach out
to the ones I love most in America—
teenagers.*

Contents

Foreword

Dennis was a pitiful sight that day I visited him in his hospital room. Surrounding the bed was an intimidating array of machines monitoring every function of his damaged body. He had undergone a tracheotomy, so a hose was connected to his neck, enabling him to breathe. The essential oxygen rushing into his lungs was keeping him alive, but Dennis wanted to be dead.

On the other side of the bed was Dennis's weary grandmother. Anxiety was etched into her kind face. She was the one who found Dennis hanging in his room. Screaming in wild anguish, she held up his body hoping there might be enough life left to save him. He had been hanging for fifteen minutes.

His eyes open wide, Dennis stared directly at me, and though he was semicomatose, I sensed that he was trying to communicate. The portable television speaker was right next to his ear, competing for attention. It vibrated with the noise of an MTV video, nearly drowning out my words.

Six weeks before his graduation, Dennis decided to throw in the towel. He saw no reason to live any longer. As I looked at him, knowing he would be permanently, pathetically disabled, my heart ached. It occurred to me that I would never adjust to the awfulness of suicide. In my travels to over one thousand cities, I have been in similar settings, but it always disturbs me to see young lives wasted.

My Life Exposé message to teenagers, which I have given in more than twenty-two hundred public schools, is a potent thirty-minute address. It has made an impact, but I have realized it's not enough. So much more needs to be said about the suicide epidemic among U.S. teenagers. So many more answers need to be given. That's why I have written this book.

Why Suicide? is not the definitive work on this subject. It is not intended to be a textbook. But it is the urgent expression of my heart, a message of hope to the despairing teenagers of our nation. It is a plea from one who has been there, one who has endured the trauma. (I tell my own story in Chapter 2.) *Why Suicide?* may upset you, puzzle you, even provoke you. I hope it does. But, above all, my desire is to do everything possible to keep teenagers from killing themselves. If this book averts just one tragedy, the effort to publish it has been worth it.

The stories you will read are true accounts, though in many cases the names have been changed to protect confidentiality.

Read this book with an open mind. Better yet, read it with an open heart.

Jerry Johnston
Kansas City

1

"See You in Hell"

Stepping briskly to the stage, I turned to face the thirteen hundred students of Hanaford High School. Just as I had done hundreds of times before in schools across America, I began my address:

"Jay was sixteen years old when his parents found his lifeless body on the floor of his bedroom. There was a bullet wound in his head. Lying nearby was the gun he used to kill himself. There was also a suicide note. It read simply:

Dear World,
I don't want to get my hair cut.
I don't want to tend kids or see Tina at school on Monday. I don't want to do my Biology assignment or English or history or anything. I don't want to be sad or lonely or depressed anymore. I don't want to talk, sleep, move, feel, live or breathe anymore. Tina, it's not your fault. Mom and dad, it's not your fault. I'm not free. I feel ill. I'm sad. I'm lonely. One last request . . . all my worldly possessions go to Debbie as a wedding present."

9

After reciting those dreadful, haunting words, I was puzzled by the students' reaction. Usually, such a crowd would become respectfully silent and remain attentive throughout my lecture. Not the teenagers at Hanaford High School. Gawking at me in apparent disgust, they were openly disturbed by the words I had quoted. Many of the girls began to cry aloud, some sobbing uncontrollably. Several faculty members showed uneasiness and uncertainty in their facial expressions. Somehow I had said something desperately wrong. It was as if a highly sensitive nerve had been pricked by my words. But I didn't know why.

As I concluded, the audience gave obligatory but empty applause. After the principal made a few brief remarks, the student body was dismissed to the next hour's classes, and I was left wondering about the negative response I had received. Over the dull roar of students filing out, I heard someone call out my name. An obviously distressed teenager stared me coldly in the eye and demanded, "How could you have given Jay's suicide note here?"

Intrigued, I replied, "I quote that note every time I speak to students."

"Didn't you know Jay went to this school?" For a moment he hesitated, studying my face. He continued, "Jay Adams—he was my best friend, and this is one of the other notes they found next to his body." Nervous with excitement, he pulled a paper from his wallet. It had been folded nearly to the size of a matchbook. As he carefully opened the note, I could see the distinctively sloppy handwriting of a teenage boy. The note said:

Dear Steve,
I am sorry for what I have done but Robert and Mom made me think. Will your mom still have wanted us to be friends? I don't know. Tell Missy I

love her and I hope she can pass science. Make
sure you never be as dumb as I've been. Make
friends and don't let them play that tape before my
funeral.

> Friends,
> Jay

Instantly assessing the message, I realized what
had happened. Steve and his fellow students at
Hanaford High thought I had quoted the suicide
note of Jay Adams, one of their classmates who had
recently taken his life. I quickly interrupted, "Wait a
minute, Steve. The Jay whose note I quoted was not
your friend. He lived in another city. He was a different Jay."

Steve's face tightened, slightly from embarrassment I'm sure. Then he blurted out, "I don't know
why he did it. He didn't give me the slightest warning that he was going to kill himself. He was my
best friend!" Steve turned and walked away, lonely
and dejected, still grieving.

Steve reminded me of countless other teenagers I
had met in other schools, kids who were struggling
to understand the senseless death of a friend. I remembered well the hurt that ached throughout my
being when some of my high-school friends died
needlessly. That day in Hanaford High School,
watching that young man shuffle mournfully away,
I had no solace in the fact that our stories had been
confused, only a double sadness in realizing that
two young men with the same name were gone forever. But that was not the last I would hear of Jay
Adams.

Within a five-day period I spoke twenty-one times
to public school assemblies, civic groups, and community gatherings in one county. My Life Exposé
address was causing no small stir, as I revealed the
stinging reality of suicide and the craziness of get-

ting stoned and smashed. Administrators, civic leaders, parents, and students alike were responding positively to the message.

In just a few years I've been on over twenty-two hundred campuses in more than one thousand cities. I've spoken to at least 2.5 million American high-school and college students. My odyssey has taken me to every state and every social level. I've listened to the frightful stories of young people struggling to survive in crime-infested ghettos. I've seen the tear-streaked faces of teenagers who live empty lives in big houses. I've heard countless stories of wasted lives, horrid accounts of drug addiction, bizarre behavior, and suicide. Whenever possible I always talk one-on-one to the teens in my audiences. It teaches me what is really going on in this country, and it keeps me from becoming just another professional speaker. Chronicled in my mind are innumerable incidents, but none is more riveting than the story of Jay Adams.

On Thursday night of that hectic week in Hanaford, the phone rings in my associate's room. Answering it, he hears a woman's quivering voice ask, "Is Jerry Johnston there? I need to talk to him really bad. Tell him this is Jay Adams' mother." I'm unavailable, but arrangements are made to meet her the following day.

After speaking to a crowd of twenty-two hundred at the Fairgrounds Arena, we are detained by people wanting to talk. Finally managing to get away, my associate and I head for the hotel. As we greet Mrs. Adams in the lobby, it's obvious she has had a drink or two to kill the time. She is noticeably nervous, and her palm is damp with perspiration as we shake hands. We sit down in a quiet corner nearby. Without hesitation or restraint, the story of her fourteen-year-old son comes rushing forth like floodwaters through a burst dam.

It becomes clear almost immediately that Jay is not the typical teen suicide. Straight-A honor student, athletic, admired by others. Not exactly a person predisposed to take his own life. Or was he? Already I'm beginning to wonder. Already I'm beginning to ask, Why?

Mrs. Adams hands me the framed portrait of a handsome young man. The photo radiates youthful wholesomeness. The dark, piercing eyes stare out in apparent innocence. Everything about the colorful image of Jay Adams belies the fact that he is dead. It makes no sense. Or does it?

I listen intently as the ashen-faced, grieving mother continues the sordid last chapter of her son's story. She tells me how Jay did something seemingly out of character. On a fateful Thursday in September, he purchased a dime bag of marijuana and boasted to his best friend Steve that he was going to sell it. Steve begged him not to. Early on Friday, Jay arrived at school with nine marijuana cigarettes he had fashioned by hand. By morning's end, he had sold four joints. But Jay had no idea that someone "narked" on him even before the first sale. As he sat in his fifth-hour class, a secretary's voice blared over the intercom, "Please send Jay Adams to the office."

Of course, no one knows what thoughts were in Jay's mind as he walked through the halls of Hanaford High School on his way to that ominous meeting. Most puzzling of all is why he didn't discard the five joints that remained in his pocket. Chances are Jay was deceived into believing his flawless academic standing would protect him.

The assistant principal interrogated Jay, searched him, and found the five joints. He had no alternative but to fulfill his responsibility and call the police. In Hanaford, as in most cities, that is standard procedure when dealing with a case of narcotics possession. The authorities were on the scene within a few minutes. Jay's stepfather, who had been contacted by the school office, arrived as the officer handcuffed Jay and led him out to the patrol car. Irate yet saddened, the stepfather followed in his own car on the way to the police station. After completing a maze of paperwork and answering what seemed an interminable list of questions, Jay was detained on the narcotics charge. A short time later, he was released to the custody of his parents. Jay was also notified that he had received a five-day suspension from school.

Her voice choking with emotion, Mrs. Adams then describes the confrontation at home that Friday night. She refers to it as a "four-hour, knock-down-drag-out argument in the living room." It ended with Jay's weeping on his parents' shoulders, saying, "I'm sorry, I'm sorry. I've made a big mistake. It won't happen again."

An ill-fitting smile breaks the sullenness of Mrs. Adams's expression as she relives the experience for us. She tells us how satisfied she felt when they hugged and Jay apologized. As he rambled down the basement steps to his room, called The Pit, she thought everything was settled. Jay had failed, but he faced up to his failure. He appeared remorseful.

Mr. and Mrs. Adams left for their jobs early the following Saturday morning. After work, they planned to grill some steaks and put the whole chaotic episode behind them.

Jay's mother tells us about her positive feelings as she pulled into the driveway about 3:00 that afternoon. There was a sense of optimism that helped overcome the disgrace of Jay's arrest and suspension from school. Knowing that Jay would be home, she took her keys from the ignition and dropped them in her purse. She knew the door would be unlocked. But it wasn't. Struggling momentarily with

the stubborn doorknob, she became angry, thinking
Jay had violated the grounding he was given.

Cursing in disgust, Mrs. Adams took out her keys
and unlocked the door. The slight movement of air
caused by the opening of the door rustled a piece of
paper on the entryway floor. It was a note from Jay.
As she reached down to pick it up, her body was
jolted by the words:

> Mom,
> Don't go downstairs. I've killed myself.
> Jay

She ran down the stairs and into Jay's bedroom. He
was sprawled across the bed, bleeding profusely
from a bullet wound to the head. Searching anx-
iously for some sign of life, she discovered a slight
pulse. Then, in a state of hysteria, she rushed up
the stairs and bolted out the front door. Berserk,
screaming in a frenzy of fear, she cried out in anguish. Suddenly, reality confronted her. Rushing
back into the house, Mrs. Adams dialed the emergency number and shouted her plea for help.
Within moments a paramedic unit was speeding to
the house.

Clutching a tissue in her hands, slowly tearing it
to shreds, Mrs. Adams tells us the thoughts that
bombarded her brain: *Maybe, just maybe, Jay will
survive. But if he lives, will he be paralyzed? Will he
be a vegetable? Is he going to be institutionalized?*

Disoriented, her fingers numb, Mrs. Adams managed after several attempts to dial her husband's
work number. Hearing the unbelievable news,
Robert ran from the office and leaped into his truck.
His heart pounding and eyes welling with tears, he
sped home.

Waiting for the arrival of the emergency squad
and her husband, Mrs. Adams struggled to main-

tain some sense of sanity. The stairway down to Jay's room seemed to her "a passageway to terror." Her eyes are earnest as she tells me, "There was a dark and creeping fear to take even one step down those stairs. It was like some tingling evil presence was waiting for me." Trembling with paranoia in that awful moment, she felt that the house had a chilling effect. She calls it "a demonic coldness."

The paramedics found Mrs. Adams in her son's room, bewildered, in shock. Pushing past her, they began to work feverishly on Jay. Their efforts proved to be futile. Lying on the bed next to Jay's limp body were several bloodstained suicide notes. They give some clue to the mystery of a teenager's life-ending decision.

To the two classmates who sold him the dime bag and possibly reported him to the assistant principal, Jay wrote:

Jason, Duane,
You dumb ————.
If I said anything you would get me hurt, huh, Duane? Well, I've talked and you'll be away for a good period of time. I was quitting. Did you nark? Of course you did. I wrote a letter to the police.
See you in Hell,
Jay.

As he indicated, there was another note, addressed to the police.

To his older brother, living away from home, Jay left this final message:

Bruce,
What a fine time for me to decide to write a letter. I thought I'd write you. Take care of Mom and Robert. You all thought I was stronger than what I am.
Love you,
Jay

He reserved the most gripping words for his mother and his stepfather, Robert. Mrs. Adams hands me the crinkled note:

Dear Mom and Robert,
I'm sorry for what I put you through. I am empty. I just can't face my friends. I want the entire 9th grade invited to my funeral. And at the funeral, not before, play this tape. Please don't play it before, if you love me. Also, have Tommy fly down if at all possible. Love you. I'm scared!
                                        Jay
P.S. The tape is in the radio.
P.P.S. Play it at the funeral.

As I finish reading the note, I am deeply sorrowful. Before I can say anything to comfort this bereaved mother, Mrs. Adams says, "Jerry, the police just released Jay's taped message to me yesterday. They withheld it as evidence until everything was finalized." (Suicide is a crime in many states.) She continues, "The first time I heard this I was in shock. So this is really my first time to coherently listen to it. I want you to listen to it with me." Almost without hesitation I agree to her request. Since then, I've had second thoughts about that decision.

"I'll be fine," she reassures me. "I'm stronger now." But within seconds after pushing the play button, she begins to lose control. Every word from Jay's clear, pleasant voice is like a dagger to her heart. He is intelligent, articulate, but getting closer to the edge with each statement. Trying to maintain calm, I feel tears pooling in my eyes, ready to plunge down my cheeks. I am beginning to feel very nervous. So is my associate.

The tape recording continues, and Mrs. Adams is now frightening me. Though I've been through hundreds of counseling sessions and I've dealt with some highly volatile situations, this one is spooking me in a strange way. Jay's mother begins to twist in her chair, in a sort of slow-motion gyration. She groans and yelps occasionally as if struck by an invisible object. Her eyes plead with me, asking, Why . . . why . . . why?

Jay's message ends abruptly. His final words, "Good-bye, Mom," echo momentarily, then there is nothing. Only the now-subdued sobbing of Mrs. Adams.

The stretcher carrying Jay's wounded body slammed through the emergency room doors at Hanaford Medical Center. But hope was gone. Technically, he died of acute blood loss and trauma, and the death certificate indicated a self-inflicted gunshot wound to the head.

Only two hundred mourners attended the funeral service. Contrary to Jay's wishes, the tape was not played. It would only have caused greater grief, of course. And it would not have answered the question every person present was grappling to understand. Why suicide?

There are answers to this penetrating question. Some are simple and readily observable. Many are not. In the pages that follow we'll find the meaning in this madness.

2

"Dad, I'm Going to Kill Myself"

The Story of Jerry Johnston

Alone and miserable, I was sprawled on one end of the couch in our family room. No one else was home, and certainly, no one was aware that a battle raged inside me. My eyes focused for the longest time on the downstairs telephone near the kitchen. I saw it as my last means of contact before my own death. I was confused, totally goofed up, convinced there was no way out. It was as if some force was directing me down a dead-end street, pressuring me to take that final turn and end it all instead of enduring the mental torment any longer.

There was a gnawing agony that caused me to ache in the strangest way. My whole being was sick, real sick, and the feeling wouldn't go away. I know what it is to have surgery, see the incision heal slowly, and feel strength gradually return. At that point in my life, the feeling was the very opposite. I was getting worse every day. The only thing that seemed to make sense was death. My mind was transporting me to a vantage point where I saw myself resting in a coffin, so peaceful, so secure. The scenario seemed a logical and appropriate conclusion to my failed attempt at life.

I lay there on the couch, wrapped in my dad's big light blue bathrobe. From the time I came home from the hospital, I wore that ugly, oversized robe. Maybe it was an attempt to feel closer to my father, because we certainly couldn't communicate. Before my two hospitalizations, our relationship was marred by suspicion, mistrust, fights, and arguments. Whenever he whipped me, I would threaten to turn him in for child abuse. But my physical problems altered that warlike environment. I became more withdrawn, even docile. Instead of screaming at me, my parents consoled me, insisting that "everything is all right, everything is going to get better." But things did not get better.

With Mom and Dad both at work and my brothers at school, my thoughts were running wild. The antique clock on the mantel ticked with an eerie rhythm that paced my weird, almost overwhelming thoughts of ending it all. My body seemed heavy as I got up and walked over to the television. One by one I studied the family pictures displayed there in decorative frames. There was Johnny, my oldest brother, who was five years my senior. I felt that I barely knew him. Next was Jay's picture, which took me back to the time when he would sleep outside my parents' bedroom door whenever they would fight at night.

Then I came to the portrait of Jeff, the brother to whom I was closest. Staring at Jeff's image, I recalled how he introduced me to the drug scene. I could see him down in our basement, dividing the pounds of dope into nickel bags, dimes, and lids. I remembered the scales for measuring hash. I thought of his telling me about kief, a pure form of marijuana. Just two or three hits and the high was

20

supersensational. I reflected on Jeff's "sales ability" in pushing drugs at our high school. I loved him and hated him at the same time.

Coming to the picture of my brother Joel, I felt really bad. He was such a good kid to have two brothers who were "freaks." I wondered how it might mess up his future.

Finally, I found myself almost hypnotized by the portrait of my mom and dad. I asked myself what it would do to them if I carried out my plans. It forced me to think back to the way all my misery began.

The Johnston family fit perfectly the upper-middle-class stereotype. We lived in Johnson County, Kansas, the fourth-wealthiest county in the nation. My father was quite successful in his position as national sales director of a major company. My mother was an interior decorator. Our home was a beautiful residence situated next to a golf course. Ours was the country club life.

I would get together with my best friend, and we'd do crazy things like interrupting the golf games of older men, infuriating them. We'd stuff ourselves at the clubhouse restaurant and charge it to my parents' tab. The only thing I cared about was having fun and moving as fast as possible.

My dad's way of communicating was to bring home surprises. Some of the things we got were an air hockey game, a jukebox, and an electronic bowling machine. Since I was obsessed with things, I took advantage of his spoiling us. One time when he returned from a business trip, I was given a new minibike.

I couldn't talk to my parents about the real issues. They were so out of touch, so antiquated in their thinking, the very epitome of straightness. My dad with his pseudoreligiousness sometimes disgusted me. Mom and Dad were so gullible that they had no idea what I was getting into.

21

When we did go to church, it was incredibly boring. The minister was the biggest drag I had ever heard. The people seemed cold, too. I called it the First Church of the Deep Freeze. And I wasn't far off, but going to church was the socially acceptable thing to do, and we did it. I remember watching my dad take notes during the sermon. Never could I understand what he found interesting enough to write down in those little spiral notepads.

Occasionally, Dad would convince me to attend the evening youth meeting at church. He would drop me off, but as soon as his taillights were gone from view, I would leave. One time, a friend and I stole some money from an elderly woman's purse at church, picked up a couple of girls, and split to have some real fun.

At school I sized up the situation almost immediately. There were two dominant student groups. The "jocks" were the more athletically inclined. They loved to drink. Then there were the "freaks," the kids who did drugs. I got mixed up with the latter group. Every day before and after classes we would hang out at a place right across the street from the school—in fact, it was called Across the Street. They were a wild bunch, but they made me feel very welcome and I liked that. Many of the kids would hit on joints until seconds before the final tardy bell. None of the faculty members ever came over. Some were probably afraid to, but most seemed downright apathetic. More than once I heard snide remarks about "poor little rich kids" and "dumb dopers." And it was true.

Now I can see that a dangerous rebellion toward authority, particularly toward my parents, began in those days. The "friends" I hung around with were turned on, and they were eager to convert me to their way of having fun.

Profanity and loose speech became my new language. My friends became more important than my "old man" or "old lady." I grew in defiant boldness, unafraid to tell my parents to shut up, get out of my room, or leave me alone. Every day I added new bricks to the wall I was building between us. Their "fault" was that they were straight, I wasn't, and I condemned them for being so out of it. I didn't want anything to do with them.

Living in a world of turned-on friends led to serious problems at school. I mouthed off to one teacher and was permanently ejected from her class. At the all-school, antidrug assemblies I would sit up in the bleachers and ridicule the speakers. While one expert told about the nastiness of drug addiction, I joked to my friends, "If we could get that guy high, he would see how much fun he's missing." By the end of the school year, I had been kicked out of five of my seven classes. I was even thrown out of study hall.

Five hours a day I occupied a special chair in the school office. Branded an incorrigible, I was told that my days were numbered at Hillcrest. Near the end of May the principal informed my parents that I would not be allowed to return to school in the fall. He told them I was a troublemaker and a negative influence on other students. On the way home after that conference, my dad let me have it with both barrels, but his words didn't faze me.

I spent the summer hanging around with my friends, doing nothing constructive, as usual. Mostly, we lounged around the club, smoking, cussing, and condemning anything and anyone that failed to meet our high standards of coolness. I spent a lot of time wondering about my new school.

My first day at Nallwood was tougher than I anticipated. All those foreign faces walking down the hallways made me feel uneasy. It began to sink in that I knew no one and I was nobody in my new

23

surroundings. Anger boiled in me toward that stupid principal who discarded me so effortlessly. Feeling sorry for myself, I was surprised and pleased when a tall, blond guy stopped me and introduced himself.

"Hey, I'm Rob. You're new here, aren't you?" His question had all the signs of genuine interest.

"Yeah," I said, "this is my first day."

"Where you from?" he asked.

"Hillcrest," I replied, identifying my former school rather than my neighborhood.

"Where do you live?"

When I answered, "Wycliffe," his eyes brightened, and he said, "Me, too. Let's walk home together." We agreed on a place to meet in front of the school. As I walked away, I thought Rob just might turn out to be a good party buddy.

That day the school seemed so straight to me. It was nestled in a quiet residential area and looked so homey. I figured that the kids at this school weren't nearly as in tune as my Hillcrest friends. How wrong I was.

Moments after the final bell sounded, I met Rob outside. As we walked home, he told me about himself. Mincing no words, Rob said he hated his mother and father, both of whom were alcoholics. They were well off, but he had no respect for them. Rob summed up his family situation by saying he lived in a house, not a home. I would learn that he was not exaggerating. His dad was a television announcer and was seldom around.

That afternoon Rob took a different route from the one I was used to. When I asked him where we were going, he shot back, "Just follow me." I could sense the apprehension in his voice. We went to the front door of an attractive house. He rang the doorbell. While we waited for an answer, I asked, "What are you doing?" He glared at me impatiently and said, "Shut up. Just pay attention." A cute teenage girl opened the door, and Rob simply stuck out his hand, fist clenched. She extended her open palm, and Rob dropped several dollars in her hand. "Hold on," she said and disappeared into the house. Within a few moments the girl returned. Opening the door again, she handed Rob a couple of joints, smiled, and said, "Thanks. Have a good time."

Rob grabbed me by the arm, and we took off. Passing through a wooded area, Rob said, "This is a good place." He took out one of the joints, lighted it, and began to smoke.

I could tell he was watching my reaction.

Savoring the first long toke, he said, "Hey, Jerry, you ever been high?"

"No, I'm straight."

"Here, hit on this." Rob offered me the joint.

"I don't know." I was scared.

"What do you mean, 'I don't know'? C'mon, man, what are you going to do at the Friday and Saturday night parties if you say no?" His question was pointed, but he didn't pressure me any more. I observed nervously as he finished.

We stopped by Rob's house, and when I walked into his bedroom, the sight staggered me. Written in permanent ink across the wall was a giant note to his parents:

Dear Dad & Mom,
You ———. I hate your guts.
Why don't you go ——— on your self.
Get out of my life. Go to hell.
Love, Rob

At home that night I weighed the whole situation. I was curious. I was intrigued. Part of me wanted to say yes to drugs, but another part of my being cried out no! I wanted to tell my dad about it. But I knew better, because he would have come unglued and totally freaked out. Unable to talk to my parents, I made the decision to try drugs.

Three days later Rob and I went across the golf course to the house where my ex-girlfriend, Laurie, lived. I knew Laurie well. We used to make out together at night on the golf course under the stars. She was some experience. But we were there to see her sister, Michelle. She sold drugs, mainly pot. Rob bought a dime bag and took me behind some bushes on the golf course. He reached into his pocket and took out a pipe. Putting a screen in it, he loaded the pipe with weed. I took in every motion from the striking of the match to the first hit. Then the invitation came again. Rob stuck the pipe in front of my lips and said, "C'mon. Now!"

I coughed as that pot burned into my lungs the first time. But with a few more attempts I adjusted. I knew then that one time would not be enough.

Soon, all I cared for was getting high. Before the bus picked us up, during school hours, immediately after school, and always at parties, I would smoke pot. That pipe became like a trusted friend. I carried the screen to it in my wallet, removing it whenever I had the chance to get a whiff of that can't-wait-until-next-time aroma.

Doing drugs was serious stuff on weekends. We would usually go to someone's house for a let's-get-bombed party. The parents, of course, were somewhere else living it up with their own friends. Without supervision, there was nothing to hold anybody back. The music was loud and pulsating. Sometimes there would be black lights and strobes. Often the goal was not simply pleasure but performance. There was an obsession to outdo the previous weekend's experience.

One of the favorite things our group did was to sit on the floor in a circle, light several joints, put them on a roach clip, and pass them around and around.

We'd try to hit on all of them at once. The aim was to see who could stay in the circle the longest. I can still see my friends and me getting blown together and laughing our heads off.

Tragically, there was more than pot. Somebody would break out the booze, and kids would start getting stoned and smashed. It was dangerous, and everybody knew it, but no one dared to say anything. And there were even worse things. One bizarre practice popular in my day was something called huffing. It involved mainly the girls. To huff, a girl would lie flat on the floor while someone straddled her and held a hand towel tightly over her mouth. Someone would then spray an aerosol substance through the towel while the girl inhaled. It gave such a buzz that some of the girls would rip off their clothes and act absolutely crazy.

At nearly every party, sexual exploits were standard practice. In fact, some parties ended in virtual orgies. I know that many deep emotional wounds were inflicted in those times, all in the name of fun.

The party lifestyle continued for many months, and I kept looking for more friends to turn on. I got Bryan, Derek, and others into drugs. I wanted them to experience what I tricked myself into believing was ecstasy.

At one wild party I got high, really high. With my mind reeling, everything was blurred. I got the munchies so I asked Rob to help me get something to eat. He gave me a plate full of unbaked breakfast rolls and some junk food items. I ate all of it.

Rob's dad picked us up about midnight. Sitting in the backseat of their car, I started coming down. My high was turning into a raunchy low. Feeling as if my insides were coming apart, I vomited all over the backseat. The car came screeching to the curbside, but even before it was fully stopped, Rob threw open the door and shoved me out. I lay there on the grassy easement, stunned and sickened. As I at-

27

tempted to raise my body, my arms were rubbery with weakness. As ordered by his father, Rob picked me up and pushed me back into the car for the remaining blocks to my house.

It took every ounce of energy for me to make it to the front door. My parents were waiting up for me as I staggered in.

"What's wrong?"

"Nothing." I said it indignantly.

"Are you sick?"

"Just leave me alone." Refusing to even look at them, I pushed by and dragged myself up the stairs to my room.

The following morning I felt no better. In fact, over the next few days I became nauseated every time I ate. When I complained to my mom, she took me to our family doctor. He ran a battery of tests and discovered the source of my problem. I had a bleeding ulcer. The doctor had me hospitalized that same day.

Laid up in the depressing grayness of that hospital room, I ached with loneliness. The first ones to come and see me were some of my druggie friends, but they weren't concerned about me as a person. One of them said, "Jerry, you've got to get well so you won't miss out on the parties and the fun." I thought about that, and it occurred to me for the first time that there was nothing worth living for. You get high; you come down. Drugs don't answer any questions or solve any problems. They just cloud them out temporarily. Afterward you're still empty, unfulfilled, searching for something more.

Coming home from the hospital was a strange experience. I wanted things to be better, but I was doubtful they could be. There waiting for me in the front yard were my brothers. They were all on their best behavior, treating me as if I were a fragile vase. Nobody wanted to say the wrong thing. "Everything's going to be great!" somebody announced.

28

But inside, I was tormented with thoughts of suicide. Like a pesky wasp, the temptation kept buzzing in on me. Frightened at what I might do, I wanted so much to blurt it out to my parents. But I couldn't. Everyone was happy to see me out of the hospital, and my bringing up something negative like that would ruin the atmosphere. It was all so artificial to me.

The physician prescribed Valium and sleeping pills to help me through the recovery period. They were an enemy in disguise. I lived in a drug-induced stupor, depressed and despairing. Already thin, I lost even more weight. I got no exercise, nor did I want to. By the time I woke up each day, everyone was gone. The awful thoughts continued to plague me. Many times I would hang my head and cry. If I did away with myself, everyone would be better off, or so I reasoned.

Reviewing the pictures of Mom and Dad and my brothers, I came to my own portrait. *It wouldn't make any difference if you were gone*. The idea seemed so brilliantly simple. Reaching deep into the pocket of Dad's bathrobe, my fingers wrapped tightly around the bottle of sleeping pills.

Kill yourself. Do it now. Take the pills and go to bed. It was late morning. Surely I would be dead before anyone got home. I held the bottle more firmly, as if it were a choice ticket to a big event and I was just about to enter the turnstile.

I walked to the kitchen entryway and picked up the telephone receiver. Slowly, mechanically, I called Dad's office. He answered in typical fashion.

"Johnston," he said gruffly.

"Dad, this is Jerry. I'm going to kill myself."

He began to weep, trying desperately to maintain control.

"We'll do something. Son, please hold on. What can I do?"

"Nothing, Dad. It's all over. I'm sorry. My friends

29

are gone. I'm sick. I'm all alone. I'm going to do it."

"Listen, Jerry, I'll be right there. Hold on. I'm coming home now."

When Dad arrived, I was freaking out, losing my balance totally. He rushed me to the emergency room of St. Luke's Hospital.

I stayed at St. Luke's for several days, enduring one test after another. The internists were perturbed about my condition, since I showed no signs of improvement. At checkout I weighed just sixty-eight pounds.

Back at home I spent eleven long weeks recuperating. I progressed from liquids to a bland diet. But still those weird thoughts were there. I fought them by reminding myself that soon I'd be enjoying good times with my friends again.

While I struggled back to normalcy, something really significant happened, though I didn't realize it at the time. My brother Johnny became engaged to Teresa Barnes. Teresa was a refreshingly likable person, and the whole family was pleased with Johnny's choice. She graciously but persistently invited our family to visit her church. Though we didn't belong to that denomination, and though my father actually resisted initially, for the sake of courtesy we eventually attended with her.

For reasons I couldn't sort through, Teresa's church was different from our church. Though I was still feeling depressed and dejected, I sensed something compelling about the atmosphere there. Even from my seat on the back row, I felt drawn in.

Somehow some of the kids in the church's youth group found out how mixed up I was. Without my knowing, a few of them went to my dad and asked him if I could go with them to their annual youth camp. Their insistence caused something to click in him. Later that day he approached me about the subject.

"Jerry, some of the kids at Teresa's church want you to go to summer camp with them in June." His tone was upbeat, but I could tell he was trying really hard to sound as if he wasn't putting something over on me.

"What kind of camp is it?" I asked, expressing no excitement.

"It's a Christian camp."

I thought Dad had gone crazy, suggesting something like that to me. "Are you kidding?" I said. "You think I'm going to go to some stupid monastery camp with a bunch of straights? No way."

To me, a Christian was either a Boy Scout or a grandma.

My dad knew that I needed to go to that camp, for a lot of reasons. So he decided on a friendly blackmail approach. With my birthday just a few days away, he bought me a big gift and placed it in our basement. When I came home that day, he stopped me and said, "I want to change your mind about going to that camp."

"Drop it, Dad. I said no!"

He smiled.

"I've got your birthday present in the basement. Want to see it?"

Before answering, I hurried down the basement stairs to discover what he'd gotten me. I couldn't believe it. Right there in my own home was the most beautiful professional foosball table I had ever seen. I had already reached it and was spinning the handles in anticipation when he dropped the bombshell.

"That's your birthday present . . . if you go to that camp. If not, I'll have it taken back."

I knew my dad well enough to realize he wasn't kidding. In the exhilaration of the moment I reluctantly agreed.

The camp wasn't so bad after all. I was surprised

to discover that there were a lot of interesting things to do. But every night they had a meeting in the auditorium, and I made sure to sit on the back row. On the last night of camp, a good-looking girl named Cherry came up to me and said, "Jerry, sit with me. I want you to hear the message." I wasn't enthused about hearing the message, but she was so gorgeous I couldn't refuse.

As I walked to the front of that auditorium, I'm sure I was quite a sight. I was wearing my favorite jeans (which also served as my pajamas). On the back was a large chicken claw patch. Some of the counselors looked as if they'd have a heart attack when I took my seat on the second row.

The greatest experience of my life happened that night. A man named Bob Werner spoke for about an hour, and I was absolutely captivated. In a firm, powerful way he told a story I had never heard. Because I listened to him and afterward acted on his challenge, my life was revolutionized. I went home a radically different person. The confusion and the craziness that had bugged me were gone. I started to think straight. I started to live right. I began to grow from that night on in my understanding of what life is all about. My parents were almost in shock when I burst through the front door after camp and exclaimed, "Dad, Mom, I'm changed. I feel so good. There is no more depression. I want to live." They broke down crying and have been shedding tears of joy ever since.

Later on, I'll tell you what Bob said that evening. But first we'll examine the subject of suicide. We'll take a look at the causes, the misconceptions, the warning signs. And we will zero in on specific courses of action to help people who may be contemplating suicide.

3

The Late Great
American Teenager

Dear Jerry,
As I write this letter I am thinking about suicide. I
can't get things together anymore. I've tried
everything, but it just won't help anymore. You
came to my school and spoke, so I'm turning to
you as my last hope. I don't want to die, but I
don't think hell could be any worse than what I'm
going through now. My parents don't realize what
is happening to me because they don't care
enough to look. I thought drugs would be my way
out, but really it's just been the path to more
problems. My best friend is a two-liter bottle of
coolers that I buy every Friday. Through the week
I get high before school or take the chance of my
brother walking in while I'm downing some
Canadian Mist. I know I'm at a dead end. I'm
scared, Jerry. Please help me.
Barbara

The flaming reality of letters like this one from
Barbara singes my heart. I wish they were rare oc-

currences, but such gut-wrenching messages come to me sometimes by the bundle. Each one is unique in style and substance, but whether neatly typed on fine stationery or scribbled on notebook paper, most say essentially the same thing: I'd rather die than live like I'm living.

The horrible truth is that suicide is America's second greatest teenage killer! According to the National Institute of Mental Health, eighteen teenagers per day kill themselves in the United States. Every eighty minutes another teenager takes the suicidal plunge. What a nightmare it is to realize over a hundred teenagers per week kill themselves in our country. In a year's time, the total comes to a staggering sixty-five hundred lives lost. Multiply that amount by the people directly affected by suicides—parents, family members, friends, classmates—and the actual dimension of the tragedy is even more overwhelming. Those left behind are perplexed and saddened, left only with the burning question, Why?

Reliable sources now say that over a thousand teenagers try unsuccessfully to kill themselves every day! Almost one teen per minute tries to commit suicide, desiring to extinguish a hurt-filled life. Many of the attempts, of course, are not intended to be lethal—they are cries for help, pleas for attention. But even in such cases, thousands of teens every year permanently maim themselves in botched attempts. Consider just one example I learned about in the following letter:

Dear Jerry,
My name is Terri. I have seen you two times in the last couple of years. I'm writing you for a very good reason and I'm sure you would relate to it well. Monday evening about 6:30 P.M. my boyfriend of five years shot himself in the head with a shotgun. Blood tests showed toxic amounts

34

of barbiturates in his system and also pot. I have noticed a difference in him especially in the last six months. His family situation is very, very unstable.

On Monday Troy went for help on his own. Two main-advertised drug and rehabilitation centers turned him away. Therefore he thought he was rejected and did what he did. Troy is going to need a lot of extended plastic surgery. His whole mandible bone has to be replaced. He has only two teeth left and he has no nose. Here is a picture and the darkened area is what is missing. He has the chin part and bottom lip. He doesn't have but half of his tongue. When he first went into the emergency room they said he probably wouldn't be able to see again or talk. He is trying to say yes or no very hard. He is beginning to open his eyes a little. We have asked Troy if he wants to live and he shakes his head yes. Respond back to me as soon as you can.

Terri

However one measures the statistics, the fact remains: Young people are killing themselves. Some drastic action is called for to deal with this serious problem. The clock is ticking away right now for thousands.

Many experts believe the problem is much more severe than the official statistics reveal. It is known that many coroners will not rule a death suicidal if there is no suicide note. Yet only a small percentage of suicidal people leave anything in writing. On many death certificates, suicide is disguised, sometimes intentionally to protect insurance benefits or to shield a family from embarrassment. After all, in our society, a stigma clings to suicide.

One official government report states:

Suicide statistics based on death certificates probably understate the true number of suicides for several reasons: 1) inadequate information on which to

35

make a determination of suicide as the cause of
death; 2) certificate error or bias; and 3) lack of
awareness of a suicide because a body was never
recovered, e.g., drowning after jumping from a
bridge.[1]

So, the analysts aren't satisfied, and frankly, I'm not
either. For example, I believe many fatalities in sin-
gle-car automobile accidents are actually suicides.
Some homicides, too, are thought to be invited by
the victims—that is, a suicidal person may put himself or herself in a position to be killed.

Make no mistake about it, suicide is epidemic
among teenage youths. In Jefferson County, Colorado, eighteen teenagers killed themselves between
January 1985 and June 1986—eighteen deaths in
eighteen months! Bryan High School in Omaha,
Nebraska, earned the dubious nickname Suicide
High when three students who vaguely knew one
another took their own lives in a five-day period.
Four other students at Bryan attempted suicide but
survived. In Plano, Texas, eleven teenage deaths in
sixteen months stunned that city. When I spoke at
Plano East High School toward the end of that suicidal chain, the students listened intently because
they had felt the eerie brush of death.

If we look at the problem in broader scope, there
are two interesting facts to observe. First, the
majority of teenage suicides in the United States—
almost 90 percent—are white, middle- to upper-
middle-class youths. Second, from 1950 to 1980,
there was a 278 percent increase in teen suicides,
moving it from fifth to second place as a cause of
death.

When you consider *all* ages, the preventable act
of suicide is clearly seen as an acute epidemic. The
Centers for Disease Control in Atlanta has revealed,
from carefully researched data, that every twenty

minutes someone (reflective of all age groups) commits suicide in the United States. According to death certificate information by the National Center for Health Statistics and from the U.S. Department of Health and Human Services, this tragic "time schedule of suicidal death" was maintained from 1970 to 1980 with 287,322 verifiable suicides that occurred in the United States.

During this fateful decade of 1970 to 1980 when the suicide problem grew like wildfire, several interesting facts are now known. Referring to all ages, the Morbidity and Mortality Report stated,

> Between 1970 and 1980, almost three-fourths (72.8%) of suicides occurred among males, and the suicide rate increased for males while it decreased for females. In terms of absolute numbers of suicides committed in 1980, 70% was among white males; 22% among white females; 6% among black and other males; and 2% among black and other females. The most striking aspect of the change in suicide rates from 1970 to 1980 was the large percentage increase in rates for males in both the 15 to 24 year and 25 to 34 year age groups and the consistent percentage decreases in rates for females in all age groups except the youngest (15–24 years). Between 1970 and 1980, suicide rates for males 15–24 years of age increased 50%.[2]

The National Center for Health Statistics reported for the age group 15 to 19 per 100,000 people, 15.1 white males commit suicide compared with 3.5 black males, and 6.5 white females commit suicide compared with 1.7 black females.[3]

For females, this period progressively witnessed the use of more violent and immediately lethal methods, with less chance for intervention or rescue. The trend for young women moved away from poison (many times unsuccessful) to firearms.

37

Right now, the most popular method of suicide for males and females is firearms.

Statistically, there have been seasonal trends with more suicides occurring during March, April, and May than during other months of the year. Interestingly, this is immediately before high school graduations.

The number of unsuccessful teenage suicide attempts has rapidly grown in the last few years. Now it is at an all-time high with a thousand teenage suicide attempts per day. This figure indicates that suicide is considered as a viable alternative to youths absorbed in problems. The fact that the majority of teenagers attempt suicide in their own homes between late afternoon and midnight, when someone is likely to walk in, reflects the ambivalence of a potentially suicidal teenager. One side wants to die while the other side wants to live, but he does not know how to ask for help or is afraid to ask. If the *real* teenage suicide statistics were known, I believe the adolescent experts along with everyone else would be in a state of complete shock! So many teenage deaths are inaccurately reported.

The suicide menace has even been documented in the almost unbelieveable preteen suicide category. There are reports of young people 3 to 11 years of age who have committed suicide or made a serious attempt.

At a recent meeting of the American Psychiatric Association, a pediatric psychiatrist described children as young as two and a half years old who have tried to kill themselves. She said that many accidental poisonings and accidents in this age group may be suicide attempts.

Some prepare for death in a very adult manner. Cathy, one 8 year old, had already written on ripped notebook paper, "I want to commit sueside." And

38

she added her will: "Dana gets half of my money and the parents other half." Then she carried a heavy rock to her father and said, "Daddy, will you crush my head please."[4]

Dr. Donald McKnew, a psychiatrist at the National Institute of Mental Health and senior attending physician at the Children's Hospital of the District of Columbia, has treated three hundred depressed children under twelve years old. Dr. McKnew said, "For children under 14, suicide seems negligible, but it's this group's eighth leading cause of death."[5]

Yes, teenagers are troubled and looking for help. A spokesman for a mental health facility devoted to teen suicide crisis intervention said, "The unit's 18 adolescent beds are always filled and a waiting list continually holds the names of those waiting for space." What's more, the plague is affecting younger and younger groups. One suicide expert, Los Angeles psychologist Michael Peck, estimates that a million children a year think at one time or another about suicide. "What we are seeing now is an epidemic of suicidal communication," says Peck. "It is a way of saying: 'Someone help me.' Youth are desperate, unhappy, confused, and compulsive. They can't think of any way out."[6]

One key to unlocking the why of suicide is to understand what is really going on in today's teenage culture in America. I know what is happening among junior- and senior-high youths, but I'm afraid many adults don't have a clue. They are naive about the true nature of the U.S. teen lifestyle. Some parents have confessed to me they are willfully ignorant, usually because they feel incapable of handling the problems. Others are self-deceived into thinking their children are exempt from danger. But no teen is immune.

I spend thousands of hours every year listening to teenagers. I know the temptations they are battling, and the crushing guilt they endure once temptation has won out. There are influences bearing down on today's youths that previous generations could not have imagined. Unquestionably, the combined effect of these influences creates a climate in which suicidal thoughts can grow. Not all teenagers will have them, but a surprisingly high number will entertain the idea. Some will go all the way down that road to self-destruction.

In the pages that follow we will examine what I call the fatal factors—the negative influences that can lead to a suicidal mind-set. Some of these activities have a magnetic appeal to teenagers, but their lure can lead to danger.

4

Going All the Way

Fatal Factor No. 1

Mary, a fifteen-year-old sophomore, said, "I wasn't able to handle the pressure. I was part of a group in junior high that was into partying, hanging out, and drinking. I started to have sex with my boyfriend and it was a real downer. It was totally against what I was, but it was important to be part of a group. Everybody was having sex."

Is Mary's dilemma typical? *Life* magazine's special report on American teenagers stated, "With an estimated 11.6 million teenagers now sexually active, a few schools have begun dispensing birth control devices and establishing daycare facilities on the premises."[1] An Associated Press article on the Chicago school system said,

The city school board voted 6–5, after two hours of heated debate, to allow a health clinic at a high school to continue dispensing contraceptives to students. "Teen pregnancy is epidemic and it is our business to deal with the problem," said Superintendent Manford Byrd. "About one of every three girls at DuSable High gave birth in 1984. There is a severe problem of teenage pregnancy."[2]

A *Newsweek* magazine cover story on the teenage sexual revolution stated,

> In the absence of moral guideposts, teenagers have developed their own rules of the love game. They no longer frown on their peers if they are sexually active. Once chastity was something to be guarded or lied about when lost. Now an uncommonly virtuous teenager lies to protect the dirty little secret that she is still a virgin. There is more pressure than ever for a girl to "get it over with," as one teenager put it.[3]

I have seen firsthand this situation and have heard this same kind of sordid report from kids in hundreds of schools. It is lamentably true.

The research organization known as SIECUS (Sex Information and Education Council of the United States) revealed that one of every two boys age fifteen to seventeen has had sexual intercourse. Another study indicated that by the time young people graduate from the eighth grade (age fourteen or younger), more than 85 percent of all basic sexual information has been learned. And, I would add, it usually doesn't come from the right sources.

High-school students today are obsessed with going all the way sexually. For the majority, sexual expression is a part of sincere but short-lived relationships. It is very common for teenagers to have multiple sexual encounters with various partners long before graduation. And it's getting worse. Sharon, a senior, said, "I'd say half the girls in my graduating class are virgins. But you won't believe those freshmen and sophomores. By the time they graduate, there aren't going to be any virgins left." One seventeen-year-old Atlanta girl complained, "If you say no, you're a tease, and if you say yes, you're a slut."

In a Johns Hopkins University study the point is made that "nearly half of the nation's 15- to 19-year-old girls have had premarital sex and the numbers keep rising." Think of it! One of every two high-school students is sexually active, and in some areas the percentage is even higher. The National Center for Health Statistics reports that only one American woman in five waits until marriage to begin sexual activity.

I have listened countless times to the anguished testimonies of emotionally damaged junior- and senior-high girls, forever scarred by "good sex" that turned out to be so desperately bad. I've also heard tearful stories from guys who have failed in their sexual exploits and can't handle the embarrassment. Soured romantic relationships are a major factor in suicide attempts.

On the other hand, I've been appalled at the callous attitude of many teenage guys. Some boast about how many girls they've "laid" or "popped." This kind of if-you-love-me-let-me ego mania is deplorable because it damages deeply and can even lead to death. When I speak in high schools, I often say, "Remember, girls, no guy will ever love anyone he doesn't respect." To most girls, sex is an expression of commitment, and when they are dumped for some other erotic playmate, the rejection is overwhelming.

Sexual activity among teenagers, of course, leads inevitably to pregnancy, which in turn leads to an upwardly spiraling abortion rate. Currently, 45 percent—almost half—of teenage girls who become pregnant have an abortion. This startling figure accounts for nearly a third of the abortions performed in the United States. "Abortions seem to be most common among the affluent. 'Upper-middle-class girls look at abortion as a means of birth control,' says Myra Wood Bennett, a county health official in Southern Illinois."[4] And some girls become so despondent, wanting neither to be pregnant nor to have an abortion, they opt for suicide. Thus, two lives are taken.

If present trends continue, fully 40 percent of today's fourteen-year-old girls will be pregnant at least once before age twenty. One report adds: "The United States has the highest incidence of teenage motherhood in any Western country; 52 per thousand as compared, for example, with 32 per thousand in Great Britain."[5] In regard to the educational consequence faced by pregnant girls, two out of three drop out of school.[6] The social consequences frequently include rejection by insincere boyfriends and lovers and scorn from friends or relatives. After an assembly, one girl said to me, "My dad repeatedly calls me a whore, and my relationship to my mom is just not the same anymore."

In the black community, teenage sexuality has reached a deplorable level. "Among the underclass in America's urban ghettos, the trends are especially disturbing. Nearly half of the black females in the U.S. are pregnant by age 20. The pregnancy rate among those 15 to 19 is almost twice what it is among whites. Worse still, nearly 90% of the babies born to blacks in this age group are born out of wedlock; most are raised in fatherless homes with little economic opportunity."[7]

In every part of the country, I've discovered that parents have an aversion to talking with their teenagers about sex. Some never bring up the subject, and others wait until it's too late. (I see a strong parallel with the refusal of parents to discuss suicide with a son or daughter who is exhibiting warning signs.) I don't blink in telling parents that if they think they can avoid discussing sex and everything

44

will be okay, they are dead wrong! Blanketing themselves with the reassuring thought that it won't happen to their Susie is sheer foolishness.

Sadly, some parents actually expect their teens to be victimized, and they feel powerless to do anything about it. One mother, quoted in a magazine article, said, "Down deep, I know it's going to happen sometime no matter what I say. Is my oldest daughter still a virgin? I don't really know and the tough part is I don't really want to know." The article went on to say, "Teenagers themselves report that, for the most part, their knowledge of sex was obtained neither at home nor in school. Many say they learned about sex from friends or from older brothers or sisters."[8]

An interesting footnote to the sexual revolution among American youths is that many teens are not as knowledgeable as they think they are. A significant percentage are misinformed or unaware of the scientific facts of reproduction and contraceptives. But they are thrust into the fast lane, and because of peer pressure, they must strive to keep pace with their sophisticated friends. On the other hand, there are teenage girls who get pregnant intentionally, for a variety of reasons—some are getting even with their parents, others simply want someone to love. Whatever the intent, the outcome is seldom what the teenager imagined it to be.

"Moreover, the sexual revolution seems to have moved from the college campus to the high school and now into the junior high and grade school." Never will I forget a tiny girl who came up to me after a lecture to about a thousand teens in an eastern city. "Everybody wants me to do it," she said. Leaning down, I asked her to repeat herself. "Everybody wants me to do it," she said again. "Do what?" I questioned. "Have sex," she said with a wide-eyed expression, as if to ask, "Is it okay?"

45

Physically, she was far from maturity. I wondered how she would ever make it through high school without suffering irreparable emotional harm.

Dr. Nancy Clatworthy, a professor at Ohio State University, has studied teenage sexuality for more than a decade. She sees in the United States

a slide in moral values. There isn't any big deal to being a virgin today. It isn't one of those high value items. It is simply a question of teenagers not seeing anything wrong with it. They see it on television, in books, the sexuality is so obvious that it is just assumed as a form of self-expression.[9]

At Dunedin High School in Clearwater, Florida, a girl with a spiked haircut approached me. "They call me dyke here," she said. "Really?" I replied. "Are you gay?" She smiled and said, "Sure. I like it better with girls." I've heard similar confessions from other girls in other schools, most of whom looked straight but were far from it. It is alarming to realize that researchers believe one in every ten teenagers is gay.

I have witnessed a growing popularity of homosexual and bisexual lifestyles among teenagers. When I spoke in Lima, Ohio, one junior became so disturbed he jumped up and ran out the door. Later, he told me he was gay. His story substantiates the claim of one researcher that "gay teenagers are among the loneliest kids in our country."[10]

Many teenagers caught in this vicious whirlpool have poured out their hearts to me. Usually, their homosexual affairs begin with a guy masturbating another guy or a girl caressing another's breasts. More experimentation leads to sexual activity, and when that happens, the guilt is often cruelly unrelenting. Many suicide notes document this fact.

When I had just completed an interview on

KMBZ radio in Kansas City, one of the DJ's asked me, "Have you heard of autoerotic asphyxiation?" I responded, "Yes, and it is growing across the nation with teenagers." It has been called the American teenagers' best kept secret. In New Orleans, youths nicknamed the practice *fantasy*. In Texas, one teenager described it to me with the word *ecstasy*. This bizarre fad is practiced not only when a teenager is alone and thrill seeking, but also when psyching out at parties. Tragically, dead bodies are left hanging after having experienced an unexpected death by suffocation.

What is autoerotic asphyxiation? A report in the Journal of the American Academy of Child Psychiatry defines autoerotic asphyxia as "self-hanging while masturbating to achieve sexual gratification." Of course, a teenager engaging in this practice is not intending to kill himself. Instead a crazy pleasure is the object. In autoerotic asphyxia, the supply of oxygen to the brain is restricted, usually by a noose around the neck, as a way to heighten the pleasure of masturbation. The constriction of the neck results in heightened sensations described as "giddiness, light-headedness, and exhilaration." While practitioners of sexual asphyxia may take elaborate precautions in the belief that they will not endanger themselves, as long as they prevent actual choking, in a moment of excitement they can unintentionally apply too much pressure to their necks, resulting in unconsciousness, complete hanging, asphyxia, and death. All research says that victims are heterosexual males, most of them under twenty. They usually fit under the classification of the t-personality—the thrill seekers.

In late 1984, police in New York City investigated apparent cluster suicides. One death in particular intrigued them, and they questioned whether it was, in fact, a suicide. The parents had found their teenage son hanging, naked, in the bathroom. They also discovered semen on the floor. The police report concluded that "the victim died accidentally in sexual experimentation."

In Ohio, the mother of another teenager who died in the same manner said, "It is time to bring this horrendous conspiracy of silence to an end. Adolescents and others should be warned of the dangers of this practice. Parents should know how to detect the warning signs before more young lives are needlessly lost."[11]

Forensic pathologists have known about autoerotic asphyxia for years, but it has never been a public issue. Until now. When a death occurs from autoeroticism, it shocks families. Doctors, and sometimes even police, tend to hide the truth and protect the family from embarrassment by labeling it suicide.

The FBI estimates that 500 to 1,000 deaths of this nature occur every year in the United States. They say that most of them are misdiagnosed as suicide or homicide or else covered up by the family because of the social stigma that surrounds a sexually motivated death. According to the Metropolitan Life Insurance Company, some 250 of its policyholders die this way in a twelve-month period. There is currently no way to get an accurate count of the number of autoerotic fatalities. The code by which coroners classify these deaths contains no such category.

Massachusetts studied all adolescent suicides in a four-year period and found that hanging was the second most frequent method of death, used by 30 percent of the victims. It makes us wonder how many were true suicides and how many were accidents. One authority did comment, "I wouldn't be at all surprised if some of those hangings were really accidental autoerotic deaths."

The FBI report, a study of 132 autoerotic deaths by asphyxiation, found that many of the victims had periodically used the technique to heighten orgasm in masturbation. They had always been able to rescue themselves before death occurred—until the last time. One doctor said, "You may do it right forty times but on the forty-first, you make a wrong move and die."

When they are found, the victims may be naked or may be wearing underwear or female clothing. Often, pornographic literature is nearby as well as various rescue devices, such as a knife to cut the cord or a key to unlock the chain. A towel or cloth is placed around the neck to prevent burns and marks. Extremities are girded with ropes or chains. When discovered, victims are suspended by the neck, caught by unexpected death.

There is a sensitive area of the carotid artery in the neck that feeds the brain. By turning the wrong way, a person can become unconscious and death is inevitable.

One expert said, "The risks of sexual asphyxia are not well known and it could be viewed as no more pathological than driving a car at a high speed."

"My pleasure is closely connected with fear," said one young man who was interviewed anonymously on TV by having his features blacked out and his voice distorted. "I'm afraid of choking. In a state of fear, life and lust are compressed into a narrow space. The more pressure exerted by fear, the more vivid the pleasure gets inside."

Some researchers think that nearly all those who repeatedly engage in this behavior suffer from a psychosexual disorder known as sexual masochism. Autoerotic asphyxia fulfills a masochistic need for punishment that arises from the guilt associated with masturbation.

Consider: According to a recent survey, more

than 75 percent of teenage guys masturbate. How many of these boys will be drawn to this deadly practice?

I mention this dangerous practice not to sensationalize but to warn parents and teenagers. Parents should watch for bloodshot eyes, marks on the neck, disoriented behavior (after the young man has been alone for a while), and possession of or fascination with ropes or chains. The mother of one victim said she noticed marks on her son's neck and asked him about them. He said it was an allergy, and she thought no more about it. Until her son's death, she had never ever heard of autoerotic asphyxia. These parents called the school principal, urging him to warn other students, but nothing was done. The next year another boy in the same school died by autoerotic asphyxiation.

A fourteen-year-old Houston guy didn't know about autoerotic practices either, at least not until he got his hands on a copy of *Hustler* magazine. There, step-by-step, he learned the technique of autoeroticism. He tried it, and it cost him his life. The family sued *Hustler*, and a federal grand jury ruled that the magazine was responsible for inciting the young man's death.

For thousands of teenagers, *going all the way* ends up meaning something far different from what they expected. A sexual exploit, whatever its nature, must be seen as a potentially fatal factor that can lead all the way down the wrong road.

5

Student Enemy No. 1

Fatal Factor No. 2

A large group of teens gathered around me after I addressed the student body of Wolfson High School. One by one, they shared their frustrations and asked penetrating questions. The last one I talked to was Christy, an attractive, dark-haired eleventh grader. By outward appearances I wouldn't have singled her out as a troubled person, but when we took a seat, she burst into tears. She sobbed, "I feel so guilty. My best friend Laura is dead." I asked for the details, and Christy related the horrible story that had devastated her.

Christy and Laura were stopped at an intersection, waiting for the traffic signal to change. A flashy sports car eased up next to them, and Laura caught a glimpse of the handsome guy behind the wheel. Whispering to Christy to take a look, Laura lowered her window and struck up a conversation. Before long the man invited them to meet him later that evening on Jacksonville Beach.

They met and had some drinks together. After a

while they left the bar and strolled down the beach joking, laughing, still drinking. About 9:30 they were about to head home when the fellow asked Christy to ride with him. Christy, thinking that Laura was too intoxicated to drive, suggested, "Laura, you ride with him, and I'll follow you." But the man was drunk, too. He sped recklessly out of the parking lot.

As the late-model Ferrari he was driving climbed the J. B. Bridge, Christy said they must have been going at least eighty miles per hour. At the crest of the bridge, the car swerved into the path of oncoming traffic. There was a spectacular, head-on collision. Christy, who had been trying to keep up, arrived at the scene of the accident within seconds. She jumped from her car and raced to the viciously smashed Ferrari, screaming, "Laura, get out, Laura, get out!" But then there was an explosion, and the car burst into flames. Her friend Laura was burned beyond recognition, her body reduced to a charred mass just three and a half feet in length.

Christy, still weeping, concluded, "The kids here at school straightened up for about a week, and then everybody was back to drinking and partying." She shook her head in bewilderment. I nodded knowingly, because I've heard the same commentary many times.

It happens at least twenty-three thousand times per year, where the mixture of a bottle of alcohol with an automobile results in death. In addition, an almost unbelievable 2.5 million people are maimed each year as a result of drinking drivers. Drinking while driving is the number one teenager killer with over eight thousand young deaths annually. The National Highway Traffic Safety Administration estimates that half of all traffic deaths involve drivers who have been drinking. This points to an even greater problem—the menacing evil of teenage alcoholism.

I struggle to comprehend why few who campaign so vigorously against drunk driving dare to speak out against teenagers using alcohol. In fact, I have gotten the implication from some that "it's all right to drink, just be sure you don't drive." That's crazy, to put it bluntly. Unbelievable numbers of kids are fueling a riotous lifestyle with alcohol.

After speaking in Fort Lauderdale, Florida, one night, I was approached by a paramedic who seriously said, "Jerry, don't ever stop what you are doing. Keep warning the kids. I shot these pictures just a few days ago. I want you to have them." I guessed this young man thought I had been around enough to see about as much as there is to see. But when I flipped through those color photographs, I almost got nauseated. They mirrored a guy and a gal who were going together. They went out that final night to have fun with a bottle of alcohol and Quaaludes. The mixture was too much. As they were racing down the highway, they must have been laughing, singing, and living it up. The pictures reflected the agony and pain. The vehicle sailed over the side of the interstate and slammed into the riverbank below. The postures of those two young people, in that automobile, captured by the camera, is a sight that will remain in my mind as long as I live.

The girl's head was down by the accelerator pedal in the driver's seat. Her body was upside down and smashed around the steering wheel. Her drenched dress had slid down her body and was barely clinging to her at chest level. Her leg had shot through the windshield and lifelessly dangled outside the car. But it was her hand and arm that created such a reaction within me. She had it outstretched toward the door as if she was pleading and screaming as the river filled the car to her eventual death. Her boyfriend's body was catapulted to the backseat. His head was cocked in an unusual manner. Ludes and booze and two more young lives are snuffed out prematurely.

A bold headline in *USA Today* arrested my attention. It proclaimed alcohol as Student Enemy No. 1. The accompanying article was a brief but provocative examination of this peril.

Drinking is today's biggest problem in USA high schools, student leaders say. Tracy Knight stated, "It's really bad. A lot of my friends go out every weekend and get drunk." People are leaving parties in dangerous conditions. They're getting into cars completely plastered, laughing and singing and driving off into the night.[1]

Surveys cited by the National Council on Alcoholism show that 30 percent of the nation's nine year olds feel pressure to drink. Thomas Seessel, the council's executive director, said, "Adolescent alcohol abuse has become one of the country's most devastating epidemics. Nearly 100,000 10- and 11-year-olds get drunk at least once a week."

The most widespread drug problem in America is not the abuse of speed (amphetamines), acid (LSD), cocaine, or marijuana. Alcohol, the socially acceptable and readily available drug, is our worst offender. Today there are 3.3 million teenage alcoholics in the United States, according to the National Institute on Alcohol Abuse and Alcoholism. That's one in every nine teenagers! With 13 to 15 million adult alcoholics in America, there is little wonder why our teenagers today are relying on a bottle of alcohol to give them pleasure and fun.

A star basketball player at Sprayberry High School in Marietta, Georgia, raced up to me after I finished speaking to the school's twenty-two hundred students. Without saying a word, he grabbed me by the arm and led me behind a partition. Then when we were alone, he looked at me, with tears streaking down his face. "Jerry," he said gravely,

"I'm an alcoholic. I just wanted you to know I'm an alcoholic. I know what you're talking about."

I have had kids tell me they start drinking before school and begin their first hour drunk. Many are simply reflecting their parents' lifestyle. If a father or a mother drinks, why should the rules be any different for a "responsible" teenager? Or so the illogical logic goes. Some teenagers have admitted to me that their first drink came at the bar conveniently located in the family den. Others tell how they were introduced to booze by a jovial relative at a family get-together. Without discipline and restraint at home, many teens are doomed. Parents addicted to the bottle have no hope of helping their alcoholic children until they first get themselves straightened out.

As I left Bonnabel High School in New Orleans, I noticed an unusual display on the school lawn. It was a demolished automobile, every foot of it crumpled and crushed. The windshield was shattered, with only a few jagged shards remaining. The interior was a nightmare of ruin. A sign in front of the wreck read DON'T DRINK AND DRIVE. Transfixed by the sight, I found myself imagining the screams of those who died in the impact.

I thank God for the eight thousand high schools across America that have chapters of Students Against Drunk Driving. I wish every school had a chapter. However we must face the brutal fact that drunk driving is not a cause but a symptom. Drinking is the root problem, and until our society has enough guts to denounce it, we're going to continue to see thousands die needlessly every year.

A teenage alcoholic, like any alcoholic, commits slow suicide. The body is damaged, and years of life are reduced. Practically speaking, drinking is a suicidal act. And should the alcoholic be killed in an accident while under the influence, that, too, is suicide. If someone else's life is lost, that's murder.

6

The Lowdown on Getting High

Fatal Factor No. 3

As I walked down the steps of West High School in Anchorage, Alaska, some students shouted at me, "Hey, Jerry! Come here. This is our Across the Street." They were referring to a story I told in the assembly two hours before. I had mentioned that when I was in school, I used to get high right across from the school at a place named Across the Street. Although it was September, it was already quite cold in Anchorage. I looked at those kids, shivering in the woods, cupping joints, and passing roach clips. I thought, *What a waste.*

On Friday night of that week in Alaska, we held a rally that was open to the community. A crowd of twenty-five hundred filled the auditorium to standing-room-only capacity. The atmosphere was electric with anticipation and concern. After the meeting concluded, I was exhausted so I sat down on a folding chair at the end of the platform. Many people came to talk; some were very distraught. One of the most pitiful encounters was with a young man named Joey. High on acid, his eyes frighteningly reddened, he had to contort his mouth to get the words out. "I can't get it together, man," he said haltingly. I knew he was blown, and it made me so sad. All I could do was tell his friend to make sure he got home okay.

Joey was really no different from a thousand and one other kids I have dealt with in every state of the union. They've come to our meetings high, hallucinating, incessantly snuffing—driving the coke deeper into their systems. Some are curiously blatant. At one high school in Columbus, Ohio, a student smoked a joint during my address! Perhaps he was being defiant; perhaps he was crying out for help in an unusual way.

Nicholas came up to me on the playing field, tripping on acid, after I spoke to a crowd at Jack Russell Stadium in Clearwater, Florida. Breaking down crying, he said, "I'm sick, Jerry, I'm sick. Please help me!"

In an Iowa farming community I met Bobby, a short, stocky tenth grader. Bobby was a speed freak. While we talked, he could barely sit still. He told me that one day at school during his lunch break a pusher lured him to a cellar stairway and turned him on. By the time I met him, Bobby was hooked.

Brad, a handsome young man in a southern high school, confessed to me that his addiction to PCP (known as angel dust or killer weed) caused him to act in a bizarre, frenzied manner. His parents were so alarmed that they placed him in the psychiatric ward of a local hospital. While he was hospitalized, some of his "friends" smuggled some PCP to him. When a nurse found him, Brad was trying to flush his head down the toilet. He was not far from death, yet he still had to be physically restrained.

One expert told me his research indicates that the average American child who turns on to drugs does so at age eleven! While I was speaking in San Francisco, a nervous faculty member approached me and asked, "Mr. Johnston, are you going to speak to the elementary students in our area?" I replied, "We hadn't planned on it. We tried that in Georgia and felt it went right over their heads." She countered, "You need to change your mind. We have experienced pot smokers here in the fifth and sixth grades. They need your message!"

First Lady Nancy Reagan, in her foreword to *Marijuana Alert,* states,

> When I visited a third grade class in Atlanta, I asked how many students had ever been offered marijuana. I was shocked when almost every little hand—of boys dressed in Cub Scout uniforms and girls in jumpers—went up. As I have traveled throughout the country, this scene has repeated itself over and over again.[1]

The *Weekly Reader* recently conducted a survey of 500,000 young students that produced some disturbing results. It was reported by 39 percent of fourth graders that "using drugs is a big problem among kids our age." And 30 percent said that "the main reason kids start to use marijuana is to fit in."[2] Unlike other national surveys, the *Weekly Reader* poll focuses exclusively on grades four through twelve.

High school kids say it's a "piece of cake" to buy drugs on a campus. "Drug-free kids are feeling alone and isolated," said Robin Seymour of Youth to Youth, an anti-drug group. A survey reported 76 percent of students usually buy drugs from other students; 14 percent from a dealer near school; 36 percent were first offered drugs at ages 12–15; 16 percent at 10–12.[3]

Consider the grim findings of the National Survey on Drug Abuse:

- 20,000,000 Americans were current users of marijuana.
- 31,400,000 had used marijuana within the previous year.
- 56,300,000 had "ever used" the drug.
- 12% of youth 12–17 years of age are regular pot smokers (20 or more times in a month).
- 27.4% of young adults age 18–25 are daily users of marijuana.
- 42% of high school seniors smoked pot during the year and stayed stoned an average of three hours each time.
- Of those who smoked pot all year, one in eight were daily users, averaging 3.5 joints per day.[4]

"By the end of high school, two-thirds of American teenagers have used illicit drugs."[5]

In major metropolitan areas, drugs are as big a problem, sometimes bigger, than alcohol. In rural America, the boozing craze among teenagers still is No. 1. Breaking it down further, I've discovered in the middle- to upper-middle-class communities that cocaine is the substance of choice. In the low-income inner-city area, teenagers will use anything they can get their hands on. They've told me how they sniff gas or glue, inhale aerosol spray, even take a chance with crack. Anything to get a buzz. Of course, there are those in poverty-ridden areas who use expensive drugs, but their means of getting them is almost always through stealing.

In one poor section of New Orleans

kids grow up fast and hard. Twelve-year-old girls, pretending to be older, turn tricks to earn "chump change." Boys don prison chic—gray T-shirts and trousers—in mock defense to where they expect to end up. Violence is a part of life, as are drugs, nights without parental supervision, stays in juvenile detention, truancy and random sex among kids barely into puberty.[6]

One of every five American children lives in poverty—one in six white children, nearly 40 percent of Hispanics, and half of all black youngsters, according to the U.S. Census Bureau. There are, of course, those in these poor areas that use expensive drugs, and their vehicle to get them is stealing.[7]

When I speak to high-school students, I purposefully use colloquial terms from my days as a druggie. I use words like . . .

- *stoned* (high on drugs)
- *joints* (marijuana cigarettes)
- *hitting* (taking a drag on a joint)
- *rush* (the euphoric feeling drugs bring)
- *buzz* (the initial high experienced from a drug)
- *munchies* (the hunger resulting from taking drugs)
- *coming down* (the depression after a drug-induced high)
- *burnout* (the physical need for a more powerful drug)
- *dime bag* (sandwich-size plastic bag with a "two-finger" measurement of marijuana)
- *lid* (a "three-finger" measurement of marijuana)

. . . and the kids know. Often I can tell that some teachers are listening intently to figure out what I'm saying while the students are elbowing one another, as if to indicate "this guy knows what he's talking about."

Drugs are here to stay, I'm afraid, and teenagers are going to be tempted by them. When they give in and experience the highs and lows drugs produce, it isn't easy to get them to go straight. I agree with one authority who wrote,

By the time he's 15, your child may know more about the contemporary drug world than you ever will. Teenagers crave experience, and once they're

60

deeply involved with drugs, drug "education" won't offer anything that comes close to the actual taking of them—the instant, chemically-induced feeling that problems have vanished.[8]

The pressure on a straight teenager to turn on is often unrelenting. The inexperienced teen will likely have at least one friend who urges involvement. Drugs are in virtually every high school in America, and at one point or another, a student will be asked, "Do you want to get high?" If it's not the friend your son or daughter hangs around with, then it might later be their boyfriend or girlfriend; and for the sake of the relationship, they might say yes to drugs.

Life magazine stated,

Unfortunately, almost all our correspondents report heavy alcohol and marijuana use (in the nation's schools). "Marijuana smoking has become as common as cigarette smoking," reports Julia Kerwin from Wilmette, Illinois, "and cigarette smoking is as regular as breathing." James Goldman of Beverly Hills, California says that teenagers there use drugs "because they're fun." Says one Las Vegas teenager: "Getting high is sometimes the only way you can get through the day. And since it is so easy to get, why not?"[9]

At Mountain View High School, I received a troubling note. It read:

Jerry,
I am into drugs like 80% of Mountain View High School but if you saw me on the street you wouldn't be able to tell. I too will become a burn-out and just maybe I'll end up suicidal. No, I most definitely think I too will take that step. I could blame it on my parents for their divorce or on my

mom for sending me to live with relatives for the past five years, or I could blame it on myself for not stopping while I still can. I don't know why I can't. I feel in place when I do drugs with my friends. I am 17. I tried finding help but help isn't always there when you're being passed a joint to hit. One day you'll read about my suicide.

One of the most controversial drugs tempting teenagers today is cocaine. Coke, as it is called by many young people, was used at least once by 17 percent of last year's high-school graduates, according to an extensive survey. A national newsmagazine reported,

As thousands of teens have already learned to their families' infinite sorrow, "coke is it" in the 1980's—the most glamorous, seductive, destructive, dangerous drug on the supersaturated national black market. "There are two trends in cocaine use," says Frank LaVecchia, a former high school guidance counselor who runs a drug treatment center in suburban Miami. "Younger and younger and more and more." The plain fact is that cocaine abuse is the fastest growing drug problem in America for adults and school-age children alike. Within the next two years, more than 20 percent of high school seniors may have tried cocaine. To Amy, coke was the wonder drug, and freebasing was better than sex. "I had no morals; I'd do anything with my body for coke."[10]

The National Institute on Drug Abuse confirms 169 deaths from cocaine in 1980 and 613 deaths in 1985. The numbers keep rising as the epidemic spreads. One of the most celebrated cocaine victims of 1986 was basketball superstar, Len Bias. My friend, former pro "Pistol" Pete Maravich, told me that only one in twelve thousand basketball players makes it to the NBA. Len Bias, drafted No. 1 by the Boston Celtics, almost made it. Two days after his signing, Len celebrated with some friends by free-basing cocaine in a college dorm room. The drug paralyzed his system, inducing a heart seizure. At age twenty-two, Len Bias was dead. *Sports Illustrated* magazine's cover story on the tragedy was entitled "Death of a Dream." The article said, "He was a kid with a crooked smile on his face, a Celtics cap on his head and the world at his fingertips."[11] But cocaine ended it all.

Len Bias is just one example of sports figures and celebrities whose lives have been messed up or lost through cocaine. Only days after Bias's death, pro football All-Star Don Rogers died of cocaine intoxication. In recent years, major league baseball has been beset with cocaine-related scandal. Because sports stars are revered as heroes by American children and teenagers, we should be concerned. So severe is the fascination with this drug in some cities that seventh and eighth graders are pooling their allowances to form "$12.50 clubs" to make small "scores" of cocaine.

Americans now consume 60 percent of the world's production of illegal drugs. An estimated 20 million are regular users of marijuana, 4–8 million more are cocaine abusers and 500,000 are heroin addicts.

Studies by the National Institute on Drug Abuse find that 30 percent of all college students will use cocaine at least once before they graduate, that up to 80 percent of all Americans will try an illicit drug by their mid-20's.

Clinical studies show 65 percent of those youths dependent on drugs or alcohol are from homes where at least one parent is also hooked.[12]

Perhaps the most volatile and dangerous form of cocaine is also the cheapest. It's called crack. The National Cocaine Hotline estimates one million Americans in twenty-five states have tried this deadly drug. "Smoked rather than snorted, a single hit of crack provides an intense, wrenching rush in a matter of seconds. 'It goes straight to the head. It's immediate speed,' says a former addict. 'It feels like the top of your head is going to blow off!'"[13] Crack costs a mere ten to fifteen dollars per pellet.

What other drugs are being used? The following are some favorites:

Speed and its chemical relative Ecstasy (MDMA) are dangerous psychedelic drugs. The truth is, they produce not ecstasy but madness. Dr. Ronald K. Siegel, a psychopharmacologist, said of the drug's effect: "I've seen people get ecstatic and I've seen people crawl into the fetal position for three days."[14]

Downers define themselves. These drugs, which include Quaaludes (called ludes), produce a low mental state, as if one's mind is in a cloud.

LSD, known as acid, is a potent hallucinogenic drug. In common usage it is wiped on a piece of candy, on the back of an envelope, or on a perforated stamp. Having fallen out of prominence, LSD is now making a fateful comeback.

Realizing how damaging and deadly drugs are, I am amazed that some organizations promote their legalization. The most vocal is the National Organization for the Reform of Marijuana Laws. NORML (an ingeniously contrived acronym) exists for the primary goal of legalizing marijuana. Founded in 1971, NORML has attracted an enthusiastic following of pot smokers. No backwoods organization, it is a sophisticated lobbyist group that potentially can bring great harm.

Many teenagers involved in the drug scene have told me of their delight in reading *High Times* magazine. Usually, they buy it in convenience stores because their parents will not allow a subscription to come to their homes. *High Times* is a magazine for drug growers, pushers, and users. In its pages are articles that provide drug-growing tips and information. There are many ads for special lights used in growing marijuana and offers for synthetic drugs. Readers can even purchase rolling papers, pill-boxes, T-shirts, and other paraphernalia with the *High Times* logo printed on it. Incredibly, each issue includes a column on Trans-High Market Quotations, which lists the prices of pot, hash, cocaine, LSD, and other drugs at their current rate in different countries. *High Times* is nothing more than low trash.

A large number of teen suicides are drug related. One report records the disturbing truth:

> According to the Surgeon General's Report, *Healthy People*, American teenagers are the only age group in the United States whose mortality rate has gone up during the past two decades. The chief reasons for this are due to drink- and drug-impaired driving, and drug-related suicide. The suicide rate among 10- to 14-year-old children has risen almost as fast as the rate among 15- to 24-year-olds. Furthermore, there are a hundred attempted suicides among young people for every one that succeeds. Suicide rates among teenagers have tripled in the last two decades—which coincides with the epidemic of marijuana use among our young people. [15]

Need I say more? Drugs have tripped too many teenagers, and a tragically high percentage have stumbled down into the dark dungeon of suicide.

Bret Easton Ellis, at twenty-two years of age, became a literary celebrity through his popular and shocking book *Less Than Zero*.[16] This book was purchased by thousands of young people nationwide who could relate exactly to his exposé of how the youths of Los Angeles' elite live. The book viv-

65

idly describes not only their cocaine addiction, drug usage, music and clubs, but also their multiple sexual encounters with one another and the same sex.

Reviewers called the book lurid, bleak—and brilliant. They compared it to *Catcher in the Rye* and more than a few focused on its vivid staccato, MTV-like images. It is a voice so full of sour ennui, so matter-of-fact in its chronicling a generation coming of age but already spent, that "a couple of privately owned bookstores in the Midwest banned the book," Ellis says, seeming half-proud, half-uncomprehending. In fact, he wishes people would read it as "a cautionary tale." "It's a sort of warning like when you are given all this freedom and there's no meaning attached to it, no sense of thankfulness. The apathy leads to decadence. I would hope people wouldn't think I'm advocating this lifestyle."[17]

It may seem difficult to wade through the explicit profanity and chilling scenes that Bret describes, but I concurred exactly with the scenario he drew of today's youths. He has been called the "voice of the new lost generation."

7

Rock 'n' Role Models

Fatal Factor No. 4

I do not believe the contemporary rock music culture is leading alarming numbers of young people to commit suicide. But there is no question in my mind that the lifestyles, philosophies, and lyrics of some rock stars are a damaging influence on American youths. Consider the astounding impact of rock performers in general.

Bob Geldof's 1985 brainchild, Live Aid, was a megaconcert without equal. Conducted simultaneously before seventy-five thousand fans in Philadelphia and ninety thousand in London's Wembley Stadium, Live Aid was seen on television by an unprecedented 1.5 billion viewers—nearly one-third of the world's population!

Thriller, Michael Jackson's biggest hit album, won sixty-seven gold and fifty-eight platinum awards in twenty-eight countries on six continents. At last count, Jackson had earned more than $66 million in royalties from that one production.

Bruce Springsteen's Born In The USA tour was

performed before five million fans in eleven countries. Ticket sales alone totaled $90 million. *USA To-
day* reported, "Springsteen's final L.A. show had
fans near hysteria. The *Los Angeles Times* ran
2,500 classified ads—the most ever for a concert—
hawking $17.50 tickets for up to $300."[1] Album
sales of *Born In The USA* have topped thirteen million copies.

Teenagers today are totally tuned in to rock music. Ours is the age of MTV, big concerts, flashy albums, gaudy T-shirts, and much, much more. But
I'm deeply concerned about some things in the rock
scene.

Rock music, without question, is as strong a stim-
ulant as some drugs. I know teenagers who spend
almost every available hour of television time glued
to MTV. Its allure is amazing. And how do the leaders of this new movement see their influence? One
of the up-and-coming VJ's (video jockeys) states,
"At first, we were trying to figure out role models.
Now we're of the attitude, 'Let's get wild. I think it
works.'"[2]

"MTV's audience has grown from 2½ to almost
30 million, the company's moved into bigger and
better offices and the videos themselves have gone
from simple concerts to million-dollar glitzy produc-
tions."[3]

Rock comes in many varieties, from mod to pop to
punk to heavy metal. There isn't one category under one label. Styles differ, and the substance dif-
fers. And some of that substance is poisonous.

People magazine dared to ask in a cover story, Has
rock gone too far? The article focused on the heated
issue of rock porn and the phenomenal influence of
certain performers and their lurid lyrics on teenagers today. *People* asked simply, Is the message of
some songs demented and vulgar, propelling youths
into an anything-goes lifestyle? Are these songs

that praise sex, Satan, drugs, and violence contaminating young minds? Do they breed rebellion?

The crescendo of concern led to the formation of a national organization devoted to establishing a ratings system for the music industry. Parents Music Resource Center (PMRC), directed by Susan Baker, wife of Treasury Secretary James Baker, is trying to persuade record companies to adopt a lyrics rating system similar to the one used to rate movies. The suggested code is V (violence), X (profane or explicit lyrics), D/A (drugs or alcohol reference), and O (occult themes).

Rolling Stone magazine reported,

> Stanley Gortikov, the president of the Recording Industry Association of America, said that screening 25,000 songs a year was impossible. Yet, fearing opposition to the PMRC would thwart legislation granting royalties to the recording industry on the sale of blank tapes and tape recordings, twenty-four record companies agreed to place a label reading "Parental Guidance: Explicit Lyrics" on their products.[4]

As the issue gets more and more media attention, people are starting to listen more closely. And they don't like what they hear. Judas Priest's "Eat Me Alive," which describes oral sex at gunpoint and leaves no room for creative interpretation.

There's more. The PMRC singled out the following:

- Prince, most notable for "Sister," a song about incest, and more recently, "Darling Nikki," a song about masturbation, on his *Purple Rain* album, which has sold more than nine million copies and collected several Grammys and an Oscar.

- Sheena Easton, whose "Sugar Walls" single, written by Prince, invites physical gratification.
- Twisted Sister, whose video for *We're Not Gonna Take It* shows a rock-loving son throwing his father into doors, down a flight of steps, and through a window.
- Motley Crue, whose song "Ten Seconds to Love" describes a quickie encounter.
- Cyndi Lauper, who in "She Bop," has some masturbatory moments of her own.
- David Lee Roth, whose Van Halen video, *Hot for Teacher,* depicts a shapely high school instructor stripping down to a bikini in front of her class.[5]

The battle lines are being drawn as performers join forces to oppose any attempt to rate lyrics. A number of rock artists have formed Musical Majority whose purpose is to fight any ratings system. Members include Cyndi Lauper, Don Henley, Lionel Richie, the Pointer Sisters, John Cougar Mellencamp, Don Johnson, Tina Turner, Olivia Newton-John, and Bruce Springsteen.

Even more disturbing than the scorchingly sexual lyrics are those that deal with death and suicide. Here are some examples:

- AC/DC's "Shoot to Thrill" tells listeners to pull the trigger for a super thrill.
- "Kill Yourself to Live" by Black Sabbath is a ballad of hopelessness and despair. Though the lyrics do not promote suicide, the title implies it.
- Blue Oyster Cult's video, *I'm Burning for You,* shows a young man who kills himself by setting his car on fire while he stays inside, burning to death. This group also produced *Don't Fear the Reaper,* which describes the suicide pact between young lovers.

- Eddie and the Cruisers sing "This old world has let you down and it's time to move on."
- The group Loverboy sings "Teenage Overdose," a morbid tale about looking for an overdose.
- The Pet Shop Boys perform a video that shows a gun pointed to the head. The song "West End Girls" tells listeners they are better off dead.
- Elton John's "Somebody Saved My Life To-night" is about a depressed boy who tries to kill himself at 4:00 in the morning.

In March 1982, seventeen-year-old Alan Stubbs ran a hose from the exhaust into the family car. At approximately 4:00 A.M., Alan died while listening to "Somebody Saved My Life Tonight."

Most well-known of all the controversial songs is Ozzy Osbourne's "Suicide Solution," on the album *Blizzard of Oz*. The lyrics describe the internal aching of someone locked inside his home away from a pain-inflicting world. The song paints the picture of a person lying on a neatly made bed, moaning with despair. The actual statement, "Suicide is the only way out," is sung in a suggestive way.

After listening to Osbourne albums for several hours, John McCollum, nineteen, killed himself with one shot from his father's .22 caliber pistol in October 1984. He was wearing stereo headphones when his body was discovered. John's grieving parents filed a lawsuit against Ozzy Osbourne.

Osbourne, formerly with the group Black Sabbath, has done things that defy understanding, things incredibly offensive. He has bitten the heads off bats and doves, urinated on the Alamo, and defecated in hotel flower pots! Trying to explain away his weird behavior, Osbourne said,

I was fighting my drug addiction. I was miserable! Because I was drugged out of my head all the time, I didn't know what the ———— was going on. It was a physical and mental torture. In the past, if I had a day off like this, I'd get up and go straight to the drinks cupboard and get smashed all day. On that *Bark At The Moon* tour, I was insane. I didn't know what I was doing. I couldn't remember anything. When I first got involved with rock 'n roll, I thought the equipment was a bag of drugs, a crazy attitude, and a wild party at the end of the gig. That's what I honestly believed rock 'n roll was. It was killing me and I wanted to die.[6]

Regarding the lawsuit filed against him by the McCollum family, Osbourne stated,

First of all I feel very, very sorry for the boy's death. It was never my intention to write a song to cause anyone harm. But I can't really feel guilty about anything because it's absurd. It's like you leaving me now, getting in your car, getting killed in a car wreck and blaming me because you came and visited me to do an interview. If those people were to actually read the lyrics to *Suicide Solution* they would realize it couldn't be further away if it tried.

It was written about Bon Scott, AC/DC's lead singer, who drank himself to death. The word "solution" doesn't mean "way out." It's "solution" meaning "liquid" alcohol. "Wine is fine but whiskey's quicker, suicide is slow with liquor"—and I've lived through that life for years and I know what I'm talking about! Most alcoholics at the end of the day commit suicide because they can't find a way out.[7]

However, on a "West 57th Street" television interview Jack McCollum, commenting on his son John said, "You see a perfectly normal kid there who doesn't show any signs of depression at all—happy. Then six hours later, he's dead. Nobody can explain it. The only thing we know is that he was listening to this music."

72

Mr. McCollum and his ex-wife, Geraldine Lugen-buehl, were sadly disappointed when they lost their case against Ozzy Osbourne. Los Angeles Judge John Cole, who ruled against the parents, expressed his opinion of Ozzy's musical style. "Trash," declared Cole, "can be given First Amendment protection, too."[8]

Perhaps this was Osbourne's intention when writing "Suicide Solution," but young listeners don't know that. There is no question that the song for some has been an incentive to death.

Though regarded by many as the sleaziest, Ozzy Osbourne has plenty of competition in the raunchier-than-thou category. Consider the facts about these performers:

David Lee Roth. Formerly with the group Van Halen, Roth is now on his own, having been replaced by Sammy Hagar. He is an outspoken rocker who talks about Van Halen with disdain. Roth is unconventional and unbridled. *Life* magazine reported how his group spotted cute girls from the platform during the concert, and roadies made sure they were given special backstage party passes.

Roth summed up his philosophy: "I can't see making a life-long commitment to one woman. 'Cause when I do I'll have had so much practice at being unfaithful it'll be a snap." He knows that he's got the audience going, especially the girls, when they start throwing their panties up to him. The show wouldn't be complete if David didn't say, '—— — the concert—let's go across the street and have a drink.'"

Prince. Prince Rogers Nelson is from Minneapolis, Minnesota. He has become very rich in just a few years. His film *Purple Rain* grossed over $80 million, and ticket sales from his thirty-two-city tour brought in $30 million more. For three years, Prince wouldn't give interviews. Breaking his silence, he said, "I'm still as wild as I was. I'm just funneling it in a different direction." He has produced eight smash hit albums and a second film, *Under the Cherry Moon*. His sensual lyrics have come under sharp attack.

Madonna. Called the most exciting female star in rock today, Madonna has been assailed for corrupting young people. One of her famous fashion accessories is a belt buckle that brags Boy Toy. Her impact is astonishing. The star of *Desperately Seeking Susan* and *Shanghai Surprise*,

> she has been the subject of much scandal, but that only seems to make more girls "wanna be" her. First, it was discovered that she had starred in a soft-porn, low-budget film, *A Certain Sacrifice*, in 1979, in which she played a sort of downtown dominatrix. At last, her belly button, and much more, could be yours for $59.95.[9]

Madonna's trademark is her bare navel, burlesque wiggle as she dances across the stage. *Penthouse* and *Playboy* featured page after page of her in the nude. Commenting on the photos, she responded, "I'm not ashamed of anything I've done."

Thousands of young Madonna Wanna-Be's have attended her concerts, where she once performed in see-through lace and fingerless gloves. One of her earlier songs, "Like A Virgin," mocks virginity. It promotes the idea that even though a girl has had sex, she can "feel like a virgin" when the right guy comes along.

Another of her songs, "Material Girl," advises girls to sell themselves to the highest bidder. "The boy with the cold, hard cash is always Mr. Right."

She is no fluke. Madonna's super-smash album, *True Blue*, in just a few weeks following its debut on June 30, 1986, sailed to the top of the Billboard charts and became No. 1 in every major country that tracks record sales. In less than three months, over three million copies of *True Blue* were purchased in the U.S. alone, making Madonna Warner Brothers' hottest artist. "Live to Tell" and "Papa Don't Preach" became two top singles from the album.

Madonna has a seemingly unerring fashion sense. She remodeled herself after Marilyn Monroe, and so teenagers throughout the U.S. and Europe followed her lead. Commenting on her new look, eleven-year-old Christy Murray of Pearl, Mississippi, said, "I'd like to look like her. I think she looks glamorous with short hair. I like the way she does her face now because she's prettier now. I've got a pair of black pants like her last video. But I don't have the top. I can't fill out the top."[10]

Young people like Christy want to be just like their star. Madonna is no flash in the pan. As a lyricist, actress, and musician, she is here to stay. She is a major influence setting the philosophy and style that millions of children and youth gullibly follow. From a small New York apartment, Madonna has gone to international success.

Commented *Rolling Stone*: "She did acknowledge her quasi-tawdry past on stage at *Live Aid* when she kept her jacket on throughout one of the hottest days of the year. 'I ain't taking ——— off today,' she announced, disappointing millions."[11]

Boy George. His real name is George O'Dowd, and he was raised in a suburb of London. When George was a high schooler, he was rejected by many of the students because he told everyone he was gay. At age fourteen, George frequented Shaguarama's, the infamous gay club. A year later, he showed up at school with his hair dyed bright orange, an act that in part led to his expulsion.

When George first began performing with the group Culture Club, audiences unaccustomed to his sound and looks would yell, "Queer!" But to the surprise of many, Boy George went on to international success. He has sold millions of recordings around the world and has appeared on magazine covers from *Rolling Stone* to *Newsweek*.

Because George is a gender-bender, the question of his sexuality has come up repeatedly. His former companion and alleged lover, Marilyn, is a transvestite with whom he had been sexually involved since 1978. Said Culture Club drummer Jon Moss (another one of George's sexual lovers),

> He did it! He opened the door. Duran Duran went there before us, but he actually opened the doors. I mean, imagine America accepting what, supposedly to them, is a transvestite—but he's the biggest star in America at the moment, right? A guy who wears makeup, is effeminate, sings songs about men. Wow! y'know, Wow! That's an achievement.[12]

Michael Rudetsky, an American musician and producer who was George's close friend, was found dead of an overdose in his London mansion where his fans had etched their tribute on the wall encircling his home, "George, you are my drug."

A book devoted exclusively to Boy George's career says,

> Culture Club are the pop phenomenon of the 80's. Boy George has become the spokesperson for a new generation, a generation that knows no boundaries of age, taste, class or sex. Boy George is the first genuinely androgynous pop star. He appears to be neither boy nor girl, but some indeterminate, invented sex between. The "Boy" of his name came about when there was evidently some confusion about his gender and he just got tired of being referred to as "her." When asked now whether he is gay, he states simply that he is bisexual—he likes both men and women. In an interview with *Gay News,* Boy George said, "Look, I fancy women and I fancy men. I'm free to do whatever sexual things I want to do."[13]

"I am partly gay. I am bisexual, and I am proud of it. Anything I can do to help the cause I will."[14]

In the summer of 1986 Boy George made news again when he was arrested on drug charges. Subsequently, he admitted, "You don't have to be a doctor to look at me and know I am dying. I am an out-and-out heroin junkie with an eight-gram-a-day habit."[15] Slowly, the Boy's career has been slipping and his last two albums have all but bombed.

Motley Crue. A group that owes much of its success to radio and MTV attention, Motley Crue is made up of Vince Neil, Tommy Lee, Nikki Sixx, and Mick Mars. In 1984 this band was voted the No. 1 rock act in the United States by *Hit Parader* magazine.

The *Heavy Metal Bible* said about them,

> The Crue isn't in it for the money, though, they are in it for the girls. Their tour bus carries a sign that says, Girls Wanted. Nikki especially likes fat girls, because they'll do anything. He likes to chew women's lingerie and is known for making any woman who wanted to board the tour bus get naked first."[16]

Motley Crue's second album, *Shout At The Devil*, exudes what they call a take-no-——— grab-some-——— attitude. Nikki Sixx said, "We are sleazy, and we like it that way." The band's emblem is a demonic pentagram, giving credence to the suspicion that they are satanists.

Consider the record of Crue's lead singer, Vince Neil. In December 1984, he drove his Ford Pantera head-on into a Volkswagen, killing his passengers, Hanoi Rocks and Nicholas Dingley, and seriously injuring the two occupants of the other vehicle. Neil was charged with drunk driving and vehicular manslaughter. Ordered to pay $2.6 million to the victims, he was sentenced to two hundred hours of community service, five years of probation, and thirty days in jail.

Perhaps the best summary of Motley Crue's life-style is the following explanation from Nikki Sixx:

> We're a rock 'n roll band. We love rock 'n roll excess. And it's beautiful. Anybody that says that they wouldn't enjoy it is lying to themselves. It's the most exciting thing to happen since Christmas. You never really have to grow up. You really never have to make your own bed. You never ever have to worry about anything except rolling over and dialing room service and stumbling down to the hall and doing what you love to do best. That's playing rock 'n roll. Then you have food, drink, and the parties back stage with all the beautiful ladies and meetin' fans and it's a gas, and then you're off to another city. "Sick" to me is daily life. I could tell you stories that would make your skin crawl about things we've done and seen. We're the guys in high school your parents warned you to stay away from. That's what we're like on stage and off.[17]

Twisted Sister. They've been called heavy metal maniacs. Dee Snider, Jay Jay French, Eddie "Fingers" Ojeda, Mark "The Animal" Mendoza, and A. J. Pero comprise this bizarre group. Says one report,

> Snider is especially scary with his huge mass of blond ringlets and the menacing and mean sneer that is always on his heavily-painted face. Dee looks like something from a cheap horror movie, especially on one of Sister's album covers—where he clutches a piece of bloody animal meat, munching on the raw bone. Other Sister anthems include *Burn in Hell* and the infamous *S.M.F.*—Snider's tribute to his fans, a group of "sick ———!"[18]

Ratt. There are five members of the Ratt-pack. Committed to a grueling schedule combing Amer-

ica's highways and beyond, this provocative group
has risen from oblivion.

> They're young, they're rebellious, and life is, for
> them, one big party. One of their favorite pastimes is,
> of course, women. The boys love 'em, and can't get
> enough. The Ratt tour bus is known as the Love
> Bus, and the Rolling Hilton—that says it all! In fact,
> one member described the biggest benefit of suc-
> cess as "good lays." He, always the rogue, looks for
> new girlfriends and new drugs.[19]

Other groups. In the heavy metal camp there are
a host of groups, many of which stretch the meaning of the words *bizarre* and *radical.* Some of the
biggest acts are Quiet Riot, Iron Maiden, Dio, Scor-
pions, Def Leppard, Krokus, Dokken, Bon Jovi, Me-
tallica, Kiss, and the new Van Halen.

A connection exists between hard rock and satanism. Richard Ramirez, accused in the sixteen Night
Stalker slayings, was obsessed with satanic themes
in AC/DC's 1979 album, *Highway to Hell.* The album cover depicts a band member dressed as a
devil, while another wears a pentagram-shaped
pendant. Ramirez's favorite song was "Night
Prowler." The lyrics describe a person sleeping
naked in bed as a prowler sneakily slips through the
window of a house. In Ramirez's case, that is exactly what happened.

The Night Stalker victims were shot, blud-
geoned, or stabbed or had their throats slashed.
Ramirez, charged with the murders, is believed to
have entered just as the song describes. Pen-
tagrams—five-pointed stars associated with witchcraft and devil worship—were painted on walls in
some of the victims' homes.

Interestingly, in Ramirez's hometown, El Paso,
Texas, the *El Paso Times* carried a front-page story
under the headline, "Fad or Fanatic Cult? El Paso
Teenagers Lured Into Devil Worship." The article

tells about a fourteen-year-old girl who thought she was at a regular party with classmates and some of their friends. When she would not participate in some of the activities, a group of girls converged on her and started beating her. She cried for help from one of the adults, but the man encouraged the fight to continue. "I didn't know they were all Satanists," she said after being released from the hospital.[20]

Sue Joyner of the WATCH Network—a national organization devoted to tracking negative influences on youth—comments: "From personal testimonies, and what we have seen, we believe Satanism is aimed at young people. Many look at it as a fad. On the contrary it is a growing movement."

Hard rock music albums and sacrificial animal remains are among the relics people have found at what appear to be occult ritual sites. Florence Luke, director of the El Paso Hotline, said some teens who have been counseled live in great fear that the devil is trying to kill them. "The animal sacrifices and the drinking of blood is very real to the children. Most of them can't even sleep at night. Some of them have thoughts of suicide and thoughts of killing others," Luke said.

Investigator Jay Arms said he found a fourteen-year-old girl among eleven youths who were conducting a satanic ritual in the sand hills near the city dump east of El Paso. "I walked up to them, after I had seen enough, and took the person I was keeping under surveillance," Arms said. He added that the youths, who appeared to be fourteen to seventeen years old, "had just skinned a dog."[21]

W.A.S.P. Another rock group to be watched is W.A.S.P. (We Are Sexually Perverted). W.A.S.P. is stinging teenagers with the poison of perversion. To study their portrait is to see depravity personified. There they are, in leather and studs, with one grabbing his crotch. Burned into their expressions is the scar of meanness. Motley Crue has been called tame compared to this four-member group of Blackie Lawless, Randy Piper, Tony Richards, and Chris Holmes. They are dangerous!

The first single by W.A.S.P. was "Animal (———— Like a Beast)"—a song so profane the record company at first refused to release it. The obscene record sleeve featured Blackie's codpiece covered with blood. Lawless insists that W.A.S.P.'s jagged anthems are a safety valve for frustrated teenagers who are hassled by parents, teachers, and the various other things that plague them. The kids are able to get it all out and have a good time, he says.

The boys of W.A.S.P. do something really frightening during their performances. During a song called "Tormentor," a nearly naked woman is brought onstage, spread-eagled, and tied across a rack. Her face is concealed by a hangman's hood. Blackie, using an optical illusion, takes a sword and sticks it through her neck. Blackie calls this "his shock-and-stun mission—accompanied by the sounds of ripping metal and explosive crunches."[22]

Imagine a teenager, high on drugs, taking in these scenes, feeding his mind on these lyrics, imitating these performers. Is this normal? *People* magazine displays a photograph of Vince Neil and a voluptuous blonde in a Kalamazoo, Michigan, hotel room bed. Vince is naked, barely covered by a sheet, and the teenage girl is cuddled next to his body. She made it with her idol. Is this success?

But what happens later?

Picture with me the empty concert hall. The floor is littered with more than trash. In one of the rows is Joey, face down in his own vomit. Joey's "tripping" was too much. He believed the trash that these performers preach every night. Who will take Joey home? Who will explain to his parents why he hates them for no reason? How will his grandparents begin to comprehend a new teenage philosophy that says, "Hate those closest to you, tell your family to drop dead."

It's all such a sham, such a clever lie. But the stars are not the losers. They laugh all the way to the bank. They build bigger houses and buy more expensive cars. Poor, gullible, ripped-off teenagers! Who are the losers? As Joey sits back down, after receiving his diploma at the graduation ceremony, he has that "dazed" expression. He is graduating from high school a burn-out. Yeah, it's pitiful, Joey is the loser.

The post-concert parties are beyond description. Jenny is high with Bob as they speed away into the dark night. Along the way home, they stop in a se-cluded spot. Now, they're in the backseat, having sex. Jenny has only been out with Bob a half dozen times; but it all seems so cool and appropriate. On the way to their love spot, they have reflected how tough the concert was. "These guys," referring to the performing group, "are studs—man, they are cool," Jenny says to Bob. Jenny is sixteen. If only her parents could see her now. Bob is all over her. He's turned on. But, later when Jenny tells Bob she's pregnant, he rejects her. She's really at a stale-mate now. Of course, it's go-get-an-abortion. Who will take Jenny to the clinic? Bob? Of course not, a cab or Jill, Jenny's friend. Her parents don't know why she's so pale and sickly on the evening of her abortion. They console themselves, thinking she has her period. But, now Jenny's tormented with guilt and pain. Bob's gone and Jenny's alone.

Just remember, Jenny, the stars say move on to another love, another sixty seconds of thrill and sensation. But, in the back of Jenny's mind, she re-alizes this is false. There has got to be something more.

8

More than a Game

Fatal Factor No. 5

Ellen got into Dungeons and Dragons when she was fourteen. "It's the most exciting thing I've ever done," she told several friends.

By the time she turned fifteen, Ellen spent every weekend playing D & D. Occasionally, it left her so fatigued by Monday morning she would stay home from school. Her parents became understandably concerned about her obsession, but she wouldn't quit playing. "Just leave me alone," she insisted. "After all, it's only a game."

Ellen never celebrated her sixteenth birthday. In Dungeons and Dragons she received the punishment of banishment from her kingdom and could never return. Ellen was so distraught she took an ornate sword she purchased from an antique store months earlier and thrust it through her body.

"After all, it's only a game," she had said. The words still ring hauntingly in the memory of her grieving parents.

I have talked with many teenagers hooked on

D & D. I say "hooked" because I'm certain it's psychologically addictive. Like Ellen, they are convinced "it's only a game," and they tell me how great it is. As I listen, they sound like freaks describing the high they get from a drug.

I am not alone in being disturbed about the consequences of D & D and other mind-bending games. A growing number of parents, educators, and even teenagers are seeing the dangers. At least one major lawsuit is now in the courts against the makers of the game, charging them in the death of a teenage boy.

What, exactly, is Dungeons and Dragons? D & D is a complex role-playing game manufactured by TSR Hobbies of Lake Geneva, Wisconsin. Introduced in 1974, it is now the favorite activity of nearly four million people. A high percentage of D & D disciples are teenagers. For many players, enthusiasm for the game becomes a mania. That can spell big trouble, leading even to a suicidal mind-set.

Dungeons and Dragons is the best known of a new generation of games called by the experts FRP—for fantasy role playing.

> They were first introduced to students on college campuses in 1975. At first these games were little more than an obscure diversion enjoyed by relatively few. Today they have virtually become a national pastime. Beginning with estimated sales of $150,000 in 1975, sales had skyrocketed to an estimated $150 million in 1982—and sales are still soaring. Although FRP games rank behind their electronic competitors, they have become popular amusements for millions of people. [1]

Nothing about Dungeons and Dragons remotely resembles most games aimed at age twelve to adult. Its cellophane-wrapped package does not reveal the usual game contents of board, playing pieces, or printed cards. The basic D & D set contains two booklets. They cost about ten dollars, but they barely get one started. To play the game well, at least four other books have to be purchased, ranging in price from eleven to fifteen dollars.

Forbes magazine, chronicling D & D's spectacular business success, reported that the game surged in popularity first among college students who were science-fiction buffs. Then the average age of the players began to drop significantly. By 1980, sales to those in the ten- to fourteen-year-old bracket accounted for 46 percent, and 26 percent among those fifteen to seventeen.[2]

How is the game played? D & D calls upon the imagination of the participant. There are no rules, only some basic guidelines. An important aspect to realize is that players have no absolutes, no boundaries. This game, as a fifteen year old told me, "helps us to extend ourselves further into the vast limits of creativity and imagination. We live in an entirely different dimension from other people. It's a constant challenge, and we never know how it's going to end."

With D & D there are no time limits. There are fantasy trips, war-game exercises, drama and psychological acting out, and the player goes from one episode to another. A single game could extend indefinitely. I have been told of teenagers who would not allow a game to end, continuing it for years. Yes, years. Most of the time, D & D lasts only a few hours. But when compulsion sets in, there is no telling what will happen or how it will end.

The game requires a minimum of four—a dungeon master and three players. The pivotal role belongs to the dungeon master, usually a more experienced player who controls the game and acts as arbitrator. The dungeon master designs problems for the players and assigns to them the strengths and weapons they can use to defeat enemies, achieve power, and gain treasure. The dungeon master makes or provides maps, combat tables, and monster lists and then guides the fantasy.

Each player selects (or receives by a roll of the dice) a character to play. Some of the roles are cleric, druid, fighter, thief, assassin, and magic user. Each character has assigned strengths or weaknesses in six principal categories: intelligence, dexterity, strength, creativity, charisma, and wisdom. These qualities enable players to know how their characters will respond in certain situations and how effective they will be in defeating the monsters.

Each character searches for a treasure, of which the location is known only to the dungeon master. The strategy involves a cooperative effort by the players to overcome the challenge of dungeons, mazes, secret rooms, and a variety of dragons and monsters.

This may sound quite harmless. The really serious problem enters when players identify excessively with their imaginary characters.

"I learned," said Allen, "that the more I played the game and learned about my character, the more I tried to be the character. After a few months, the character became me at the other times in my life. It was like I developed this other person inside of me and he talked to me all the time. When my character died one night, I ran home, crying all the way. For three days I didn't want to talk to anybody because I thought that the real me had died."

On the fourth day, Allen attempted suicide. The timely intervention of his worried parents saved his life.

Part of the D & D ritual includes service to a patron god. Players can choose their god from an interesting assortment including Egypt's Ra (the sun god), Osiris (god of nature and the dead), Vishnu (the Indian god of mercy and light), and Varuna (the god of order and the protector of oaths).

The *D & D Players Handbook,* published by TSR Hobbies, reminds players that "swords and sorcery best describe what this book is about." The *Handbook* also states that D & D "is so interesting, so challenging, so mind-unleashing that it comes near reality."[3]

John Eric Holmes, a science-fiction and D & D fan, says that part of the game's fascination "is watching our alter egos grow and develop as our imagination goes to work." He acknowledges that when one of these alter egos is killed in the game, the player may suffer psychic shock and go into depression. "My players know I hate to see their personae killed . . . I usually provide reasonably easy alternatives to death, like wish rings and resurrection."[4]

Some people may willingly accept such an explanation and even admire Holmes's approach. I don't buy it. As one who has dealt with numerous teenagers whose thinking has been screwed up by fantasy role-playing games, I oppose them for several reasons. Using the example of D & D, I'll name three.

1. *In Dungeons and Dragons, players put themselves under someone else's control.* The dungeon master (sometimes called the referee) makes final choices and decides the way the game will go. Although the dungeon master is supposed to be neutral, even proponents of the game admit this could be a problem.

Byron Pritzer, a spokesman for TSR Hobbies, casually dismisses criticisms. When asked what would happen if the dungeon master who sets the boundaries of the universe for every player was evil, he said, "I suppose that could happen, but it really isn't likely. The purpose of the dungeon master is to be neutral, strictly neutral. The only real requirement is that he produce the most colorful, fanciful game possible."[5]

In a midwestern city I talked to twelve-year-old Jennifer, whose best friend, Angie, had taken her own life. She brought up the subject of Angie's (and her own) D & D involvement. "I got scared all the time because I knew he [the dungeon master] wanted to get rid of Angie. And she kinda knew it, too, but she kept thinking that she was smart enough to figure out how to win."

2. *In Dungeons and Dragons, players learn to delve into the bizarre and the supernatural.* Irving Lee Pulling was a talented high-school sophomore who was really into Dungeons and Dragons. At school one day while he was playing the game with some other students, a curse was put on his character. Irving became sullen and depressed. When he got home, he took a pistol and shot himself through the heart. He was only sixteen when he died.

Irving's parents attempted to sue the school, but the court ruled against them. They now have a $10 million suit pending against TSR Hobbies. The Pullings maintain that their son's suicide was the result of following precise instructions found in the Dungeons and Dragons game. They believe their son concluded that the way to remove the curse was to offer himself as a human sacrifice.[6]

D & D, like other fantasy role-playing games, transports the players into the environment of medieval witchcraft. The producers would tell you this is simply for effect, but I believe differently. I see a direct and deadly connection, an encouragement to participants to learn the realm of the supernatural.

3. *Dungeons and Dragons teaches an immoral lifestyle, without regard for others' values and needs.* Bart's parents took their seriously depressed son to a psychiatrist. He admitted his addiction to D & D, explaining, "The more I played the game, the more I wanted to get out of this terrible world. Every time we played we committed murder, arson, robbery, and even rape. Everything is bad, just bad, and I can't stand much more of it."

Some proponents argue that teenagers playing D & D and other fantasy games are no different from children playing cops and robbers. What they neglect to point out is that it is understood that the cops are the good guys, standing for law and order. The robbers are the bad guys and expect to be brought to justice. No such concept exists in D & D or similar games. Rather, players are allowed to win by any means so long as they win. They use their wits and strengths to achieve power and wealth. They have no value system. Good only triumphs if the players have more power, sneakier measures, or more ruthless tactics.

The so-called Freeway Murders in southern California in the early 1980s were commited by an obsessive Dungeons and Dragons player. He was so preoccupied with the game that it became his life. He turned his room at home into a medieval fantasy world. At times he put on makeup and dressed like his character. Apparently, the game also entered his real world when he chose to race down the freeways, shooting and murdering people in other cars.[7]

The murderer in California is not an isolated example. Critics of fantasy games, including the National Coalition on Television Violence (NCTV), have linked the game to twenty-nine suicides and murders since 1979.[8]

In 1985, the NCTV petitioned the Federal Trade

Commission and the Consumer Protection Agency to require TSR Hobbies to put warnings on game books stating that the game has been linked to several deaths. They have also asked the Federal Communications Commission to require similar warnings during the airing of a cartoon version of the game shown to children on Saturday mornings.

Although all three agencies have rejected the request, the NCTV vows to continue the fight. Pat Pulling, mother of Irving Lee Pulling who took his life because of the influence of Dungeons and Dragons, formed another organization called BADD (Bothered About Dungeons and Dragons). She says, "D & D manuals contain detailed descriptions of killing, satanic human sacrifice, assassination, sadism, premeditated murder, and curses of insanity. Much of the material comes from demonology, including witchcraft, the occult, and evil monsters."[9]

Teenagers in all parts of America have come to talk to me about their involvement in Dungeons and Dragons. They bring me their books, their patron deities, their stories. And all of them bring their fears. Most say the same thing, that it began harmlessly enough but then led into hours and hours and more and more submersion. One girl said, "I couldn't think for myself anymore. It was like praying to this thing to know what to do. It was awful."

The more I research, the more I learn about the long-term effects of fantasy role-playing games. They are, unquestionably, oppressive mind robbers. Rather than free the imagination, they imprison it. But, above all, I detest them because they ultimately rob some young persons of life itself.

Though I have focused attention on the danger of fantasy role-playing games in general and D & D in particular, I have other concerns. Ouija boards, for example, do not seem dangerous to most unsuspecting teens, but they are dangerous, for they lead young minds to rely on superstition and chance. And, yes, I know of teenagers who have become despondent over the outcome of a Ouija game and attempted suicide.

There's nothing wrong with diversion. I love to read a good novel or play a good game. But I'm not about to turn my mind over to somebody else. That's not diversion. It's deception of the worst sort. Don't be fooled.

Home Sour Home

Fatal Factor No. 6

Julie cried as she told me the story. She and other graduating twelfth-grade girlfriends were at a slumber party celebrating that soon school would be over and they would be free. Everybody chimed in to share their thoughts late that night as they relaxed in sleeping bags scattered across the room, but Brenda dominated the conversation. She kept talking about her problems. Not just one, two, or three. That night, all her problems spilled out. One after the other, Brenda expressed problem after problem. Finally, somebody told her to cool it and let someone else talk. After everybody eventually dozed off, something possessed Brenda. Slipping out of her sleeping bag, she quietly made her way up the stairs to the bathroom while her friends comfortably slept. Once she had locked the door, she carefully wrapped the cord of a hair dryer around her neck and hung herself from the shower rod. Early the next day the door was torn down and Brenda was found. But, as with so many others, it was too late. In our minds as we see her body jerking in the motion of strangulation during the wee hours of the morning, we wonder why. Julie told me there were problems in Brenda's family. "If we had only known that night that she was reaching out to us," she sobbingly commented.

Literally by the hundreds young people have come up to me and told me they had either already tried suicide or were seriously considering it. Some show me their scars of past attempts or detail the planned method of their self-destruction. I have always responded with the exact same question to every teenager—why? Truthfully I can say that at least two-thirds of all suicidal young people have responded to me with the word *family* in their answer as to why suicide was on their minds.

There is absolutely no question in my mind that in the home there is the potential to make or break a teenager. I am really sick of hearing the speeches about "delinquent teenagers" in our country. In reality, there are many troubled adults and extremely turbulent homes in which teenagers' problems gestate to the point of suicidal explosion.

The breakdown of the family, in my opinion, is the chief area of direct concern for finding answers to the teenage suicide epidemic. Most teenage suicides occur at home. Many also begin at home, that is, the suicidal mind-set starts to develop there. In the environment that should give security and satisfaction, everything seems to go wrong for many teenagers. Instead of peace, there is fear. Instead of harmony, discord. Instead of joy, unhappiness. And then the deadly thoughts come. For those overtaken, suicide becomes the final, grisly chapter to a sad story.

Scores of suicides and attempted suicides have no connection whatsoever to drug or alcohol abuse. But many are linked to family problems. Insightful parents and intelligent teenagers should know about the potential for this kind of danger at home. Even the best families are vulnerable in this area.

The great divide. No longer can we speak of the typical American family. In years past, that phrase described the traditional, middle-class unit of father, mother, and children living together. Today, that combination represents a minority of American homes. The combined destructive effect of divorce, remarriage, and millions of children born out of wedlock has created a far-from-ideal society. For many—perhaps most—teenagers, it is a very hard world in which to grow up and develop.

Divorce. In 1830, one in every thirty-six marriages in the United States ended in divorce. In 1970, four out of every ten marriages ended in divorce. Today, however, one in every two marriages lands in the divorce court. It is astonishing to realize there are some geographic sections of America where the divorce rate now exceeds the marriage rate. It is interesting to note that as the teenage suicide rate skyrocketed 278 percent from 1950 to 1980, the divorce rate increased as well. One relevant and reliable source indicates the number of divorces per 1,000 married women rose from 9.5 to 21.9 during the years 1954 to 1978.

In the last thirty years our society has undergone more major changes, at a faster rate, than during any other period. Someone has suggested that we are now moving from an industrial to a postindustrial or information-oriented society and that the job market and its demands have totally changed. This all presents added pressures on the family. Turbulent families, splitting apart at the seams, promote suicidal thinking. Teenagers sometimes blame themselves for their parents' problems.

Right now, there are 1.2 million divorces every twelve months in the United States—the highest in the world. Realizing there has been a rise in divorce of more than 100 percent, the proportion of teens who carry the burden of a chaotic family has increased dramatically. It is not possible to overstate the trauma on teenagers when they watch two parents—whom they equally love—split apart and go their separate ways. When divorce occurs, teenagers are often hard-pressed to cope with the demands. Their loyalties are strained because, in most cases, they don't want to fail either parent. Caught between a father and mother who have rejected each other, their own sense of worth totters like a drunken man on the curbstone. ABC's "Nightline" reported the suicide attempt of a teen who felt his divorced parents made him choose between them. He said, "I sort of feel sometimes that the fights that go on between my dad and mother pull me apart. So it's like I've got to choose sides. I can't—it's difficult for me to just stay in the middle and be pulled from side to side." Another teenager interviewed on the same program said of her parents, "they can't help me. They're children themselves."[1] With an estimated one million young people each year experiencing divorce and separation, we see a contributing reason to youth suicide and attempts.

Remarriage. Trying to replace an original parent where there is a bond of love with a step mom or dad is, to some teenagers, impossible. Adapting to a new parental figure can get extremely complicated for a teen. In some cases, the stepfather or stepmother does not truly accept the teenager, who is a reflection of the original parent no longer in the home. Getting up and going to bed every day in this awkward, unacceptable environment may invite suicidal thoughts. "Our home is all screwed up now. It will never be the same again. I would rather go back to the fights my original parents used to have than this. Why not kill myself?" one teenager thinks. Some remarriages have worked beautifully, but many have completely bombed out. Researchers tell us that 75 percent of divorced persons remarry within a few years. Adding this group of people to other remarriages resulting from the deaths of spouses, it is calculated that about eight million children/young people in this country now live in stepfamilies.

According to one estimate, if present rates of childbearing, divorce, and remarriage continue, as many as half of today's children could be involved in stepfamilies as child or parent sometime in their lives. So we are not talking about a small problem!

Blended families. Commonly, remarriage brings with it not just a stepmom or dad, but step-brother(s) and sister(s) who are immediately in the social network of the teenager's life. What a major adjustment! *Psychology Today* stated,

> According to recent research, 17% of remarriages that involve step-children on both sides wind up in divorce within three years—compared with only 6% of first time marriages and only 10% of remarriages without step-children. The special stress involved in step-parenting brings about the striking early divorce pattern.

Some couples try having a child together to unite their families more strongly. But having "yours, mine, and ours" doesn't work either, and for many, divorce is inevitable. Picture the teenager, trying to develop socially, going through puberty, caught in this web.

Single parent families. According to the U.S. Census Bureau, 12.6 million children under the age of eighteen live with only one parent; that figure represents 20.1 percent of all children. It is easy to see what natural problems are presented in the single parent home. Because of the parent's need to put bread and butter on the table, the teenager does not have the natural accessibility to the single parent who is working. The pressure of needed finances is there. Also, the absence of the other parent, whether it is father or mother, leaves the teenager deprived of a balanced development. In some cases the single parent has multiple short-lived romances with the opposite sex. The teenager viewing this activity becomes confused, and personal insecurity is a by-product. Romantic interests of a parent become a major threat and can be viewed by the teenager as real competition. This can later become an ongoing problem if a remarriage results.

Undeclared divorce homes. In millions of two-parent households, there is undeclared divorce, and the children inevitably sense the division. Mom and dad are together legally and practically, but not emotionally. Countless teenagers have told me through tears about the friction between their parents. And for some, they are sure of the cause: themselves! Dr. Steven Stack, associate professor of sociology at Auburn University, pointed out that research on the families of teen suicide victims indicates they are more likely than other families to be characterized by recurrent yelling, less affection, a pattern of hostility, nagging parents, a symbiotic relationship between parent and child that permits no autonomy, intolerance of crises, depressed and/or dominant mothers, neglect of children for a career, too much or too little discipline, and geographic mobility that breaks up social networks.

The chaotic family increases psychological states amenable to suicidal behavior: depression, guilt, anxiety, hopelessness, low self-esteem, and so on. For example, years of hostility between parents can

leave the child emotionally deadened, lagging behind his peers in psychological development.[2]

There is no question that problems in the home
are carried by a teenager internally and leaves them
plagued with questions about the validity of life.
One woman in Ohio handed me a poem she wrote
about a neighbor family whose son committed suicide. She told me she watched the family deterio-
rate through several years until the son's suicidal
death. When he was young the family was closer,
but eventually things changed. Her poem high-
lighted three areas of the young man's life: elementary school, junior high, and college. It read:

Once on yellow paper with green lines
   He wrote a poem . . .
And he called it "Skip"
   Because that was the name of his dog and
   that's what it was all about . . .
And his teacher gave him an "A" and a gold star
   And his mother pinned it to the kitchen wall
   And showed it to his Aunt.
And that was the year that his sister was born
   And his parents kissed all the time . . .
And the little girl around the corner
   Sent him a postcard signed with a row of x's
And his father tucked him into bed every night
   And was always there.

Then on white paper with blue lines he wrote
   Another poem . . .
And he called it "Autumn" because that was the
    season
   it was and that's more what it was all about.
And his teacher gave him an "A" and told him to
    write
   more clearly.
And his mother told him not to hang it on the
    kitchen wall

Because it had just been painted.
And that was the year his sister got glasses and
  His parents never kissed anymore
  And the little girl around the corner
  Laughed when he fell down with his bike.
And his father got mad when he cried to be tucked
  in.

On a piece of paper torn from a notebook
  He tried another poem
And he called it "?" because that was his big concern
  And his professor gave him an "A" and a
  hard searching look, and his mother didn't say
  anything at all because he never showed it to her.
And that was the year he caught his little sister
  necking
  on the back porch and the little girl around the
  corner wore too much make-up so that he laughed
  when he kissed her—but he kissed her anyway.
And he tucked himself into bed at three in the morning with
  his father snoring soundly in the next room.

And that's why, on the back of a matchbook cover he
  tried another poem . . . and he called it
  "Absolutely nothing" because that's what it was all
  about.
And he gave himself an "A" and a slash on each wrist
  and hung it on the bathroom door
  because he couldn't make it to the kitchen.

A big deterrent to teen suicide is a dad and mom
that have a happy relationship. You can't kid teenagers or pull the wool over their eyes. If their parents' marriage is raunchy and the home wall-to-wall
hell, they will know it. It will mar their development
and, for some, breed suicidal thoughts. I am
positive that a loving, balanced home in most cases
will be just the influence necessary to avert suicidal
disaster. It is up to the parents to instill security or
insecurity in a teenager.

Communication breakdown. Seventeen-year-old Julie felt cut off from her parents. Her final, distressing words give just a glimpse of the despair that covered her like a shroud.

Dear Diary,
No one knows I'm alive or seems to care if I die. I'm a terrible, worthless person and it would have been easier if I'd never been born. Tabby was my only friend in the world and now she's dead. There is no reason for me to live anymore.

Julie's shocked parents strained to comprehend how their daughter could think such thoughts. Did she really feel that her only friend was Tabby—a pet kitten!

Repeatedly teenagers have told me that they can't communicate with mom and dad. They say: "My parents don't know what's going on. I just don't relate to them. We can't seem to get on the same wavelength." As I listen, I realize this is a nationwide problem, not linked to certain social or economic distinctions. Communication breakdown occurs in parent-teen relationships across the spectrum of American society. One survey in the state of Texas revealed the average parent in that community spent fourteen minutes per week communicating with their teenage son or daughter! Incredible, but so true of so many families across America. It is so much easier to let the T.V. become the electronic parent or a rented video the communicator. In reality, the majority of parents I have met throughout the country want to communicate only when it is too late—after the suspension from school, after pot was found in the car, or after the trip to the clinic that proved the pregnancy test was positive. But that's too late! My message to parents is simple: Start talking now.

Ask your teenagers if they have ever or would ever consider suicide. Ask them what would be the factors that would cause them to think about self-destruction. Talk to them about sex, how far to go on a date, and what to say when their dates say, "let's make love." Bring up the issue of drugs and alcohol.

Did you try alcohol? Drugs? Sex? Were you lonely in school? Did you always have a date for the big events? What did you do on Friday and Saturday nights? Did you cuss your parents? Tell them. They will appreciate your honesty more than a hypocritical front.

Don't try to hide your problems. If you have a drinking problem, drug problem, or a marital problem, be open and frank about it. Express your desire to succeed and to get over it. Why not ask their help? Your teenager will relate more to an imperfect, flawed adult than they will to a perfect parent. Be transparent with them. Get out of naivete and gullibility and get down on the teenage level. Realize times have changed. It's no longer sneaking behind the trash bins drinking beer. It's far more serious. If your teenager makes it, it will be nothing short of a small miracle.

Let me also say, if you don't devote the time to them that prioritizes them above *your schedule*, your golf game, your business associates, your ladies' club, you might as well forget it. They will know you are a fake. Have regular times alone with them. Get interested in what they're interested in. If it's the basketball game or football game, be there. If he or she plays in the school band, go to their concerts. Remember, while you're climbing to the top, if you lose your son or daughter, you've failed, no matter what digit salary you make, how many CD's, TSA's, stocks or bonds you have.

Love them enough to do something about dis-

obedience. Giving your sons or daughters everything on a silver platter is not love, it is stupidity.
When you give them too much freedom, they will
be confused enough to think, "Hey, if my parents
really loved me, they would do something about all
this garbage in my life." Ultra permissiveness is not
the answer. When you give your teenagers too
much freedom, they will secretly want some rules.
Why? Because every teenager needs the security of
a parent who cares enough to do something about
disobedience. It shows you really care. This idea of
bringing your pot home and we'll smoke it together
is idiotic. Pawning your child off continually to a
nanny, guardian, an older brother or sister, or simply to himself, says one thing loud and clear to the
teenager—I don't care about you.

If it is feasible and reasonable, give your children
the freedom to call you anytime during the day. Let
your secretary know to break in on you anytime
your son or daughter is on the phone. Make it clear
to your son or daughter that it would be impossible
for them to interrupt you day or night.

Be informed. Find out from an academic source
what's happening at school. Read some competent
materials that give you some knowledge about
drugs, alcohol, and teenage sex. Know the facts.
Too many parents feel inadequate for their tasks as
parents and try to run away from the problems. The
best help you can offer your children is to face the
issues and to have the current information.

The following letters describe the results of what
happens when there is a fissure in the home. A
high-school student in New York named Mike
wrote me a sad letter about his family not caring
and not understanding:

If I were to commit suicide everything around me
would be better without me, and I would be better

without it. There would be no more father who wishes I wasn't born. No more [girlfriend] to get in trouble with. No more struggles to be accepted with others. And, I would be somewhere better than here, because this world is just too much for me. Well, Jerry, I guess this sort of explains why I want to commit suicide. I hope you understand. You're the only person I have been able to tell this to . . .

Eileen's poor communication with her parents almost resulted in her premature grave. She lives in Alabama now. She wrote to me:

Recovering from a suicide attempt is a long process. If my parents had only listened to me when I first talked about it, I might have been helped before I tried to kill myself. My folks knew that I was thinking of suicide . . . I had expressed my desire [to die] several times before talking an overdose . . . I suppose they might have thought it was just a stage I was going through . . . But, it wasn't a stage. I was acting out of total despair.

My parents just couldn't believe that their daughter tried to take her life. I came within minutes of death. The fifty pills I had taken had been in my system for an hour and a half before I was discovered and rushed to the hospital.

So, Jerry, tell parents to love their children as if it was the last day they could spend with them. Tell parents to listen to their teenagers. It could save them a lot of heartaches later on in life—the lives of their kids.

What causes a communication problem? At the heart of it, I believe is a breakdown in trust. Whenever trust is lessened or lost in a relationship, communication suffers severely. Teenagers and their parents can relate in a wholesome, positive way only if they trust one another. And this means there has to be room for failure and forgiveness. Let me illustrate.

A teenage girl who had sex on several occasions with her boyfriend broke up with him and confessed to her parents what had happened. Her father spouted, "All you are is a little slut anyway. That's all you're ever going to be. If you had been a decent girl, you never would have done it in the first place. Why do you tell us now? Because you think you're pregnant, isn't that it?"

That wasn't it, after all. The girl was reaching out to be consoled and understood in the aftermath of an upsetting experience. But instead of consolation, she got condemnation. She ended up being destroyed, ground up in the gears of her father's anger.

What really hurts is the realization that so many lives are lost because of poor or nonexistent communication between teenagers and parents. It doesn't have to be this way. Bridges, strong and enduring, can be built across the so-called generation gap. But it takes work, commitment, flexibility, and acceptance—on both sides.

Missy, a high school student from Texas, wrote me a six-page letter:

If we would've talked [when I visited her school] I would've told you that I have one of the best homes and one of the worst. My parents give me almost anything I want but they don't trust me. Sure, I've made mistakes that weren't too intelligent, but mother says we should forgive people who make mistakes. Why should I be around if they can't trust me? What can I do if I'm not responsible enough to make my own decisions? You know, I tried to kill myself for the first time in the 7th grade. Fourteen years old and I tried to kill myself . . .

Missy wrote of four attempts to take her life. She's a top student in her school and a high achiever.

104

The tyranny of expectations. At a 1985 high-school commencement in Waverly, Massachusetts, a graduating senior received his diploma, stepped to the microphone, and announced, "This is the American way." Then, taking a revolver from under his gown, he raised it to his head and pulled the trigger.[3] He survived, fortunately, but a dramatic statement was made.

What drives a young man or woman to such extreme action? In some cases, it is the culmination of mounting pressures—internal and external—that have been building for years. Finally, in volcanic fashion they erupt in a display of raw emotion and, sometimes, bizarre behavior.

One of the most intense pressures bearing down on many teenagers is the parental expectation level and demand for conformity. Even without knowing it, many parents attempt to cram their teenagers into a mold, using a variety of techniques. From some affluent, highly successful parents comes the pressure for their son or daughter to succeed—to make it to the very top. This could be in academics, athletics, or even dating. The mounting pressure becomes a steamroller to many young people, and suicide is their way of escape. The traditional past habits of many parents are forced on some young people. "You have got to go to Yale, Princeton, or the University—your father did," a pressuring parent says. "If you're not first-string on the football squad, you will be less than what your dad was."

In the high school years, the pressure to succeed materially comes from some affluent parents. Teenagers are told that there are only so many quality jobs out there and they had better get going now if they are going to be successful. The pressure is on to be perfect. Yet, I know young people who could care less about owning a BMW, Mercedes, or Lincoln, or wearing Polo or Perry Ellis. They are saying,

"I don't share your value system—back off." Parents need to give their teenagers breathing room and let them develop their own skills and talents.

Teen magazine cited the story of Jamie whose parents had outsized expectations. Early in life, he learned he could please them only by what he achieved. When he did well at school, they loaded him with compliments and praise. They became cold and distant when he didn't do well.

After high school, Jamie went away to one of the Ivy League colleges. He did badly and tried to explain about wanting to change schools, but his parents wouldn't hear of it. He couldn't meet the academic load and felt he could not live up to their expectations. Jamie killed himself at college and left a note for his parents that said simply, "I knew I would fail you."

One pressure tactic used by parents is promoting comparison. "Why can't you be like your sister? Your brother doesn't act like that. What's wrong with you?" Statements like these should be banned from the American family's vocabulary. They are damaging, and they can be deadly.

Another negative behavior I see is the compulsion of some parents to live out their dreams through their children. The achievements they could not attain become the brass rings toward which they relentlessly push their kids. For teenagers with any measure of individuality, this is often insulting. For those who are highly sensitive, it is threatening. More than one embattled teenager has told me, "I don't want to be like them. I can't meet their expectations." A sixteen year old said, "My parents know two words: *faster* and *hurry*."

Is anybody home? In the years following the Second World War, an increasingly larger percentage of mothers have taken jobs outside the home. Many mothers, particularly those who are single parents, have no alternative. Economic realities demand that they earn a living to meet their children's needs. For many, however, this pattern was established when the teenager was a baby. Many mothers prided themselves on how quickly they could be back to work after their newborn's birth. Subsequently, the little one was farmed out to babysitters and day-care facilities. As a result, that teenager may not have bonded with his mother when he was an infant—this is a deprivation some psychologists believe is critical in the further development of suicidal teens.

Today in the United States, there are more than seven million latchkey children—those who come home from school every day to an empty house.[4] Until mom or dad arrives, they are left to fend for themselves. Some experts agree that this is beneficial to their development, helping them become independent and self-motivated. For some kids, I'm sure that is true to some extent. But I know it has hurt many others.

Knowing friends who are welcomed by an interested parent after a long day at school, many teenagers become bitter at their own parents' absence. Television, chores, homework, even brothers and sisters are poor substitutes for a mom or a dad who is there, willing to listen, willing to care.

What disturbs me is many mothers' employment is not a technical necessity for financial survival. It is a choice to obtain luxury items and have plenty of pocket cash. Long after your teenagers leave your home, they will thank God more for a mom that was available at home than for wall-to-wall carpeting, a giant-screen T.V., and any of the other innumerable luxuries that so many people feel they cannot live without.

Young people have told me that they have sex with each other in the hours before a parent arrives.

Some have said it is a challenge for them to go all the way with a boyfriend or girlfriend right in their parents' bed.

Some mothers and fathers work so hard at their jobs that by the time they get home they are completely worn out. They are then physically present but emotionally absent. One sarcastic fourteen-year-old girl said, "Even when they're home, their heads are out to lunch. I've had pot and speed all over the house, even left birth control pills around, but they never noticed." She paused a few seconds and added, "Or maybe they noticed but didn't care." This girl gave up, slit her wrists, and lay down in the bathtub to die. Her boyfriend's unexpected visit saved her life.

The trauma of transition. The average American family moves every three years. Those who often suffer most in these times are the teenagers. They must make new friends, learn the "system" in a new school, and readjust to a new environment. When kids are very young, moving to a new city is usually not difficult. But for those in junior or senior high, it can be absolutely traumatic. The geographic mobility of many American families leaves the teenager with no extended family around him. This compounds the problem. Often, a grandparent, uncle, or aunt takes up the slack for a non-communicative parent. Leaving a close friend, boyfriend, or girlfriend behind has spurred some teens over the cliff.

Plano, Texas, is a progressive, upper-middle-class city in the northern suburbs of Dallas. It has grown from a pleasant small town of 17,000 in 1970 to a bustling community of over 100,000 today. Most of the new residents are upwardly mobile executives. Due to job promotions, many of them don't stay too long. Some of the young people have suffered as a consequence. During a sixteen-month period in

1983, eleven Plano teenagers committed suicide. In most cases, they did not know each other, and none made a death pact. But they were all frustrated, they all felt intense pressure, and many sensed an inability to fit in. Plano earned the dubious name, Suicide Capital of America. One rival football team, playing one of Plano's high school teams elevated the banner, "Kill Plano before they kill themselves." Plano East Senior High was one of the most receptive assemblies I have ever conducted.

Not far away in Clearlake City, Texas (the NASA area of Houston), a young man hung himself from a tree. His suicide note observed, "This is the only thing around here that has any roots."

Transition for thousands of teenagers means being shuffled from one foster home or detention center to another. They do not belong anywhere or experience any sense of permanence. These particular young people, I believe, need special attention. The suicide rate is even higher for kids in this category. Inevitably, families will move from house to house and city to city. But parents must be sensitive to the need to lessen the trauma for their children's sake. When it is feasible and reasonable, teenagers especially should be allowed to participate in the entire process of making a move.

The untouchables. Touching is such a simple thing, but it works wonders. It communicates sensitivity and understanding and love. From infancy we're influenced by the power of the human touch. This was proved in a fascinating study performed on newborn babies in a London hospital. One group of infants was fed from a bottle, without physical contact by the one doing the feeding. The other group of babies was fed the same formula while being held by a nurse. In every case, those who were touched developed faster and stronger and had less infection!

109

So, what does this have to do with teenagers and suicide? Simply this: Many parents, especially fathers, stop touching and showing physical affection to their children as they enter the preteen and teenage years. This can be lethal, because some kids interpret this drawing away to mean there is something wrong with them. A poignant, moving story that appeared in *Reader's Digest* includes the testimony of a forty-three-year-old mother who still ached from this kind of emotional injury. "When I was six," she said, "my mother told me I was too old to be kissed. I felt so bad that every morning I went into the bathroom and looked for the tissue on which she'd blotted her lipstick. I carried it with me all day. Whenever I wanted a kiss, I rubbed the smear of lipstick against my cheek."[5]

Parents who withdraw emotional and physical affection as their children grow older make a dangerous mistake. It can lead to deep, private heartache. And it can be one element of a fatal decision.

Dying to see you. For a child, nothing is harder to bear than the death of a parent. When that death is a suicide, the pain seems even greater. It is common for a grieving child to want so desperately to be with the deceased parent that suicide is considered. Twelve-year-old Dana Golub, from the time of his mother's death until his own suicide, thought continually about going to be with her.

Denise, a bright teenager, was shattered by the loss of her mother. Nine months later, her father remarried, which only deepened Denise's loneliness. On the anniversary of her mother's death, Denise downed a bottle of pills. She left this note to her father:

I don't want you to worry about me.
You'll find someone to replace me just

as easily as you found that woman to replace my mother.

Fortunately, "that woman"—Denise's new stepmother—arrived in time to save her life.

Whenever there is a death in the family, however it was caused, there must be open discussion among the survivors. Without a sharing of hurt, there can be no full healing.

Don't get mad, get even. Child abuse. The very words provoke a righteously indignant response, as well they should. Although exact figures are hard to come by, it is estimated that approximately one million children and teenagers are sexually abused each year and that at least half of this number have had an incestuous relationship. When a child is abused, irreparable harm can be inflicted. Abuse can be verbal, spewing forth as venom from a parent's mouth. It can be emotional, as expressed in an obvious and intentional withdrawal or neglect. It can be physical, coming in the form of vicious beatings, deprivation of food, or even imprisonment. There are many cases on record of children, teenagers included, who have been chained to beds, locked in cages, even strapped to racks!

And as I have constantly encountered from defeated teenagers, abuse can also be sexual. In Newark, Delaware, a heartbroken girl told me the sordid details of abuse she suffered. Her parents were divorced, and she was sent to live with an aunt and uncle. It seemed at first like an ideal situation. They were active churchgoers and seemed really nice. Then a few weeks after she moved in, her uncle came to her bedroom and sexually molested her. He began to make it a regular practice, and she felt powerless to do anything. As she revealed her story, I realized it was still going on! With a counselor, I went immediately with the girl to see her uncle's

111

pastor. He had never suspected that a fine, active church member like her uncle would be guilty of such hideous acts.

The sexual abuse of teenage girls by stepfathers who unleash vicious lust on them is deplorable. When children are victims of abuse, something very curious happens in their psyches. They begin to think, *I deserve this*. Once that mental mechanism is activated, it becomes more and more difficult for them to tell someone what is happening. It's for this same reason that kidnapped children, though they know where they belong, do not contact anyone for help. In the case of sexual abuse, there is the fear of causing someone—a father, a stepfather, or other relative—to go to prison. Abuse itself imprisons the child.

Convinced there is nowhere to go and no one to talk to, many abused children choose the suicide solution. One boy said, "Instead of getting mad, I decided to get even." The revenge motive in suicide occurs not only when there has been abuse. It also happens when there has been a buildup of hostility.

Home can be a breeding ground for suicidal thoughts, so parents and teens alike must be careful to keep open the lines of communication.

10

Broken Pieces
Fatal Factor No. 7

Don't worry about me because I've been talking to God for over a year now, and I am going to heaven where I will be *happy*. God doesn't like me coming home early, but he doesn't like the devil beating the hell out of my mind every day either. I'm sorry, but the devil has my mind and I must escape him before I do something wrong. Be happy for me, not upset, for I have left the devil now, and he can reach me *no longer*. I feel relief now. Wish me luck and happiness in my new life.

With these confused, fateful words, Gary ended his life. The pressure was simply too much. It is hard for some adults to understand the stresses that can build up in a teenager's mind. The burden of these stresses is like an overinflated balloon ready to explode into a thousand pieces.

Teenagers in America are subjected to severe pressure in their peer relationships. And when things go wrong, the pressure can be just too much to bear. For many it is a shattering experience. I know because I've seen the broken pieces. I've talked with teens who have been so hurt they want to run away, or be loners, or end it all.

"There is no pressure like peer pressure." That's what an exasperated sophomore named Cathy told me as she poured out the story of her troubled life. Cathy, like many teenagers I've counseled, wants to fit in but doesn't like the high price of conformity. She wants to be a part of the group, but she wonders how far it is right to go. "I really want my friends to like me, but I want to be my own person, too," she says, implying a choice of one or the other.

There are several ways in which teenagers are broken, and each one indicates a need for caution and concern. Experts refer to the *trigger mechanism*, some negative experience that is the final impetus to commit suicide. The trigger mechanism is a severe disappointment that finally pushes a teenager to the decision for suicide. As you read these words, many young people are on the verge of death. They are barely hanging on. What will be the trigger mechanism in their lives?

Dr. Aaron T. Beck, professor of psychiatry at the University of Pennsylvania School of Medicine, was asked what kind of person was a suicide. "People who have a negative image of their lives. The critical factor is a sense of hopelessness that is characteristic of people who may have gone through severe stress such as disappointment in their careers or a breakup of a relationship. They exaggerate their problem or its consequences.[1] When Dr. Beck was asked if a suicidal tendency is a family trait, he responded, "The idea may seem silly, but people do inherit the temperament that, when combined with other factors, could lead to suicide. We know this from a study of adopted children in Denmark who were reared apart from their biological parents. Among 57 adoptees who committed sui-

cide, there were 12 suicides among all their biological relatives. A control group of 57 nonsuicidal
adoptees had only two suicides among relatives."[2]

Broken dreams. People generally tend to be idealistic about relationships when they first start out.
How many people, for example, actually expect on
their wedding day that they will someday be divorced from their new partner? But marriages end
up that way 50 percent of the time in our society.
One reason this happens is that people assume that
they will always get along, that the relationship will
just naturally get better. But relationships don't get
better unless people work at them. Right relationships have to be built carefully and consistently.

A teenager is the most idealistic of all human
beings about friendship and romance. A teenager
holds the expectation that everything will always be
great, that his or her relationship will always be
close. But communication breaks down, all is not
great, and the closeness is lost. This situation can
be traumatic, especially when the teen has put the
other person on a pedestal. When a breakdown occurs, when a best friend is no longer, some teenagers become so despondent they consider suicide.

I encourage teenagers not to give up when
friendships go through rough waters. Persons who
are truly friends will be willing to work things out—
and persons who stubbornly refuse to try and readily reject the relationships cannot be trusted to be
there in good *and* bad times. Teens are better off
without "friends" like that. No such broken relationships are worth the price of life.

Broken romances. High on the list of factors that
prompt suicide attempts among teenagers are broken romances. These romance-oriented suicides
are some of the saddest, most heart-breaking stories
I have ever heard. So many teenagers feel that
when relationships bomb, so does their opportunity

for fulfilled lives. When the feelings for others are strong, and when those bonds suddenly are broken, utter hopelessness can set it. This is a dangerous time.

I spoke in an Oklahoma City high school where some of the teenagers were used in the filming of *Silence of the Heart*. This film was a gripping, prime-time motion picture that told the unforgettable story of two lovers taking the death plunge together. I will forever remember the feedback I received from students in that school following my address. To adults, the idea of killing oneself for love seems foolish, to young people it makes sense and is real, very real. For females who are dumped after having gone all the way, coping without their "eternal" love is, for many, the hurdle too far to cross. Males as well as females may feel that absolutely *no one* will ever fill the void of that perfect guy or gal.

An attractive eighteen-year-old girl from the midwest checked into a run-down New York City hotel. She'd been in the room less than an hour when she phoned the night clerk and implored, "Please get me a doctor right away. Hurry!" When the physician arrived, he found her in bed, moaning and clutching an empty bottle of barbiturates. He rushed her to a hospital to have her stomach pumped.

During a brief span of consciousness, the girl said that her boyfriend had jilted her. Her final words, recalled by the doctor, were, "They'll all be sorry when I'm dead. But if only I could have talked to somebody like you before . . . maybe I wouldn't have done this."

Suicide not only expresses hopelessness and helplessness, but also is used to strike back at parents who broke up the romance, at the other person for leaving school, and at teachers for being insensitive and for not caring enough.

To understand the revenge principle in a romance-oriented suicide, we need to think more about the nature of the romance. The first sexual encounter for anyone is the one that is always remembered. When I stand up in front of a group of teenagers and ask, "How many remember the first time you had sex with anyone?" everybody who has had sex remembers. People may not remember the tenth time or the twentieth time, but they remember the first time. They remember who and where, and many remember the clothes they were wearing.

Some young people are striking back and some are saying, "It is all over for me now." For young men, the risks seem even greater, at least statistically. Psychologists theorize that males often experience more intently than females the feeling of being rejected. Both sexes feel rejection, of course, but teenage boys especially do. Incidentally, the threat of a drastic response is greater if the relationship has gone on for a long period of time.

The teenage years are a time of adaptation, so I counsel against getting so identified with another person romantically that the teen can't function without that individual.

Broken ideals. Perhaps the most common of broken ideals is the loss of virginity. When it happens, most teenagers (even if they won't admit it) feel the ache deep within of having given up forever something very precious.

Obviously, I believe strongly in the rightness of reserving oneself sexually for one's life partner in marriage. I don't hesitate to take this stand. But I realize that many teenagers who hear me speak and read my writings have already given up their virginity. I don't condemn them, but I do encourage them: Don't think that having given it up you have to keep giving in.

This is an important issue to me because many, many teenagers have told me they wanted (or actually tried) to commit suicide after they first got involved sexually. It is, unquestionably, a fatal factor.

Broken expectations. When a friend is unfaithful, it hurts. When desires—perhaps for something really big and important—don't materialize, it hurts. When carefully laid plans fail miserably, it hurts. And the hurt can be so overpowering that one of these things can lead to suicidal thoughts.

It is important not to bank on something so strongly that if it doesn't work out, life isn't worth living. One young man told me that when he didn't get the scholarship he was *sure* he was going to be granted, it seemed as if his world had come to an end. He considered suicide. Fortunately, he realized soon that things were not that bad. He accepted his situation, got rid of the supernegative thoughts, and took another direction. Today, he's glad it all happened.

There's nothing wrong with great expectations, but there is danger when we turn our expectations into immovable objects.

Broken hearts. The most crushing blow of all is the death of a friend. Whether that death is by suicide or accident or natural causes doesn't really matter. A death is a death. It disturbs, it defeats, and it discourages. And as I've mentioned previously, it can provoke deadly temptations—suicidal thoughts.

How tragic that one person's death should lead to another, but it happens frequently. The reasons vary, and the questions are troubling: How can I live without her? Why should I go on if he's not here? Does life have meaning anymore? Why not join him now?

This brings up the whole issue of celebrity deaths and their impact. In our society, movie stars, rock idols, and other celebrities become in the minds of their fans just like personal friends. It's a strange, curious thing, but it is true. I have a few friends whose names are household words. They tell me that people regularly come up to them and carry on a conversation as if they've been lifelong friends!

Some teenagers who idolize celebrities to the point that they feel personally attached to them can't handle the death of their idol. When John Lennon was killed, numerous Beatle fans around the world committed suicide. The same thing happened in the wake of other deaths: Marilyn Monroe, Janis Joplin, Freddie Prinze, John Belushi, to name a few. It happens in other countries, too.

A broken heart—whether caused by the death of a friend one actually knows or a celebrity one feels close to—must be mended with time and reality. There's no reason one death should lead to another. When the loss occurs, it is right to grieve, right to be saddened. But it's also right to go on living.

11

The Making of a Suicidal Person

In the preceding chapters we have examined what I call the fatal factors. Each one of these activities and environments has the potential to create a suicidal mind-set. Sex, alcohol, drugs, rock music, the occult, family conflicts, peer pressures and problems—all carry the seeds of destruction. Those seeds will not take root and flourish in every individual, but they will in a surprisingly high percentage of people.

Suicidologists and sociologists refer to these as societal and relational influences. In other words, they have to do with the world we live in and the people we live with in that world. When things go wrong—in our circumstances or in our relationships—there can be a powerful, negative effect. It can lead to death-dealing thoughts.

There is also another world to be considered: the inner world. In that place—the truest, deepest part of a person's being—there can be great turmoil. Fear can lurk there, and loneliness can plant itself like a leech. And if there is a spiritual void, the individual will sense it in the secret, inner self.

When I analyze the question, Why suicide? two words sum up the attitude of the suicidal person: *hopelessness* and *helplessness*. The suicidal person feels locked in a situation that is without hope and beyond help. Looking at the problem, the individual is convinced there is no way out.

No hope.

No possible solution.

No way that anything can be really "normal" again.

No way to ever really love again.

No way to succeed in life.

No way.

This is how the suicidal person feels, and it doesn't really make sense to others. But it's important to recognize and acknowledge the person's feelings because this understanding can be the bridge by which a suicidal person can be reached.

Dr. Frederick Holliday was a brilliant man who had achieved much in his career. A graduate of Harvard, he was a superb educator and administrator. But there were problems deep inside him that others failed to recognize. After all, he was smart, he could handle himself.

Dr. Holliday, who served as superintendent of the Cleveland, Ohio, school system, got fed up with life, and he started believing the suicide lie. Finally, he took a .357 revolver and shot himself in the chest.

The two-page suicide note Holliday left expressed the despondency of his heart. He felt hopeless. He felt helpless. So he did away with himself. It was a most illogical act for a logical man. It struck his family with grief and left thousands of students stunned and wondering why their superintendent had killed himself.

In suicide there are always reasons. But none ever makes any sense, really.

What we must keep in mind is the priority not to analyze details but to avert danger. In the chapters that follow we'll broaden our understanding as we look at specific courses of action we can take.

12

Who Killed Dana?

The day before I was to address the student body of Oregon City High School in a suburb of Portland, something dreadful happened. A local newspaper account reported the incident under the headline, "Tragedy Mars Abuse Speech." The article read:

"Do you know what this is going to be about?" One Oregon City High School girl asked a classmate as they filed in the gymnasium Thursday for an all-school assembly. "Drugs and alcohol," replied the second girl. "Again?" "Again."

Before the assembly began, school principal Barry Rotrock had an announcement to make: two Oregon City High School students had been killed in an automobile accident on Wednesday.

Senior Sue Rich, and junior, Ken Krupa, had skipped school the day before and had driven to Kahnee-ta. Both were killed instantly when the car they were driving failed to negotiate a curve and ran off a cliff. Word of their classmates' death had reached students the previous afternoon, and some of the kids were still visibly shaken by the news.

123

The principal had taken a few moments with speaker Jerry Johnston before the assembly to ask him to tone down his heavy-duty message on teenage suicide and substance abuse, explaining that he wanted to avoid causing a grieving student body more emotional distress. Rotrock told students, "I think yesterday's accident makes this assembly even more important to us," and Johnston launched into his lecture with 1,450 teenagers in the palm of his hand.[1]

As if it were yesterday, I recall the intense concentration written on the faces of those students. They were nearly motionless. I knew it was an impressionable moment for them, with the horrifying thought of their friends' deaths so strong in their minds, but I did not hold back or soft-pedal my message. Having been told privately that the accident resulted from a joy ride with alcohol, I saw a crucial connection between the tragedy and my address. So did Principal Rotrock, and I commend him for the boldness to make a tough decision.

On our way to the gymnasium that brilliantly sunny spring day, he said, "We were going to cancel this assembly because of the accident. But when my staff and I talked, we realized that what happened is the very reason you need to speak."

When you make a frontal attack on hot issues such as teen suicide, alcohol and drug abuse, sexual promiscuity, and the let's-get-high philosophy, you're bound to run squarely into some hairy circumstances. I do, practically every week.

I'm not an analyst hibernating in a plush office, waiting for people to come to me. I don't go in for fancy titles or dignified introductions. And when I'm face-to-face with a crowd of teenagers, I don't hide behind the lectern reading some dry notes in a dull-as-dust monotone. I don't call my audience "children" or "youngsters." You see, I've been where many of these teens are now. I remember, and I identify.

I'm not a speaker-for-hire who makes the circuit giving a high-powered, polished message. I'm on a strict salary, and I don't personally receive any of the honorariums given for my speaking engagements. All monies are directed into our organization for the funding of extensive endeavors. We have numerous full-time employees. It's true, my schedule is grueling. I speak an average of thirty times every week and travel over 150,000 miles each year. The novelty wore off long ago. Sometimes I get fed up with hotels, restaurants, baggage claims, and especially that memorized recital by the flight attendant on every plane trip.

I have spent countless hours sitting in almost-empty auditoriums and gyms, talking to kids after my lectures. Many have come to me, often in tears, sharing their deepest feelings of loneliness and despair.

In Texas, Pam blurts out, "I can't keep my ———— together. I'm going down quick." Marty, in Colorado, rushes to the stage after the dismissal to say, "It's a hell of a lot harder living than dying." Karen, in North Carolina, shows me the court papers explicitly describing how her father had sexually abused her, forcing her to engage in oral sex. Crying softly, she says, "I feel so dirty. I don't want to live." In Virginia, Judy pours her heart out. She is a vivacious girl but says she has wanted to kill herself ever since her boyfriend moved away. "I feel so alone," she tells me earnestly.

When I speak in this nation's high schools, kids listen to the illustrations I share, and they find themselves in what I'm saying. The names in the stories might be Christy or Jay or Bill or Sandy, but I discover my listeners often insert their own names because the experiences are so similar. It's not unusual for me to see teenagers lower their heads, silently crying, because of the relevance of the message. Always after an assembly, kids mob me to ask questions and sometimes share their stories.

I'm careful to keep no professional distance between myself and those who confide in me. I've never been an informer or worked undercover for any bureau. My goal is not to turn kids in, but to turn them around. By gaining their confidence, I've gained an opportunity. Students have given me their drugs, pipes, rolling papers, and suicide notes. I've seen many scars from needle punctures and slashed wrists—grim evidence of unsuccessful suicide attempts.

I have a large stack of letters from young people who have written to say in various ways "I would have killed myself if you hadn't come to speak at my school." That's encouraging. But it's frustrating, too, because I can't go everywhere. I push myself vigorously, but I recognize my limitations.

There is one penetrating question I have been asked repeatedly in relation to my Life Exposé assemblies. It deserves and demands an answer. Usually, the question is stated something like this: Don't you think that you are putting ideas into young minds when you talk about suicide?

If it is possible to cause someone to commit suicide by simply discussing the subject, we are in a desperate situation. If that were possible, one might be guilty of involuntary manslaughter by saying the wrong thing at the wrong time. But this is not the case. Suicidologists—experts in the study of suicide—are in nearly universal agreement that talking about this disturbing issue does not prompt people to take their lives. In fact, discussion is one of the most important deterrents.

By talking about suicide, we create a greater awareness and openness, and we help the person with suicidal thoughts to realize that others struggle, too. When in the midst of crisis, many young people think that their problems, questions, and doubts are unique. One girl wrote to me:

> I always felt like no one else in the whole world ever felt this way. When you read that suicide letter, I kept thinking, that could have been my note. Those are the things I would have written. It helps to know that others think that way, too.

When someone shows signs of depression or exhibits some of the other suicide warning signals, what should be our response? Many people fall prey to the misguided notion that it's best to do nothing, to just let the problem work itself out. That can be fatal. Left alone, a teenager who is moderately or severely suicidal will usually get worse, not better. The teenager may become tightly wrapped in a cocoon of self-pity, and the silence of others serves to confirm the thoughts, *No one notices. No one really cares about me.*

It takes courage to lovingly confront an emotionally distressed teenager, but it must be done. I have tried to console more than one grieving parent who has cried out, "Why didn't I do or say something?"

Suicidal compulsion does not happen out of the blue. It builds through a long process fraught with despairing, negative thoughts. There is, without question, a predisposition toward suicide before the act occurs. Generally, it begins with the idea that life is just not going to get any better. Then, with that fatalistic lie boiling in the mind like a witch's brew, the depressed person thinks: *I am helpless to change my circumstances. The only thing to do is give up.* This sense of utter helplessness then produces an abject hopelessness, which is even worse. In that state, there is the potential for serious, suicidal thoughts.

The thought strikes suddenly, and it appears so

logical: *Why not kill myself*? Once the idea enters the brain, the predisposed person can become obsessed with it, dwelling on it for days, weeks, even months. Some suicidal people tell others what they are thinking or at least give hints. The majority say nothing, though they may express other signs. When the thinking begins to focus on the actual time and method of death, the predisposition is about to bear its bitter fruit. If not prevented, the person will go through with the plans.

I have counseled suicidal teenagers who fit every category of behavior imaginable—homosexuals, lesbians, drug addicts, alcoholics, murderers, rapists, incest victims, overdose survivors, petty thieves, bisexuals, high-society debutantes, middle-class kids, inner-city ghetto residents, pathological liars—so I know that if they will talk, others will, too. And that's what we must strive for, so that as many as possible can be saved. In every community of any size, there are teenagers whose predisposition to suicide is like a bomb ticking away inside them.

April 8–12, 1985, I spoke to thousands of students in the schools of the greater Wooster, Ohio, area. My schedule was jammed with engagements, as usual, but it did not originally include Creston Junior High. Officials of that school contacted our representative and asked if I could come to speak. The details were worked out for an address to the student body at 1:45 P.M., Wednesday, April 10.

As I entered Creston's auditorium that day, so did a twelve year old named Dana Golub. Dana had known nothing but trauma in his brief life. His father had violently killed himself. Then when Dana was only eight, his mother died of cancer. He rehearsed that devastating memory every day. Dana was moved from one place to another, living in four different homes. Finally, he ended up with twenty-four other children in the Christian Children's Home, a residence for emotionally troubled young people and those from turbulent families.

Dana talked incessantly about his mother, about how much he missed her. Repeatedly, he told others that if he killed himself, he could be with her again.

As Dana listened to me that deceptively pleasant afternoon, I have no idea what went through his mind. I didn't even know who he was, of course. A teacher later reported that when Dana returned to class, he commented on what a good speaker I was and how much he enjoyed listening to me. Approximately an hour later, Dana got on the bus that transported students to the children's home. Arriving at the home, Dana went to his room. After an hour or so, one of the social workers asked the other children about Dana. No one knew where he was, so they checked his room. Opening the closet, they discovered him. Dana had taken a belt and hung himself.

The following day I drove to Wooster, where I was to give a speech to the Rotary Club. As I was getting out of the car, our local representative rushed up to me and breathlessly said, "Jerry, a teenager who was at the Creston Junior High assembly has committed suicide!"

I was shocked. The words hit me with the insulting force of a slap in the face. My stomach clenched as if it were a fist. Stunned, I asked, "What happened?" Shaking his head in dismay, he replied, "I don't know many details, but I'll find out. I just heard the news."

At that point I had been in more than eighteen hundred schools, and there had never been such an incident. I knew there had to be a reasonable explanation.

Speaking to the businessmen of that civic group was difficult because my mind was elsewhere. I kept thinking back to the assembly at that tiny rural junior high. In my mind I saw again the wide-eyed faces of those kids as they hung on my words. I wondered which face was Dana's. I agonized to remember if I'd said anything different. Had I omitted something or misstated an important fact? Was I too rushed to answer questions?

As I reconstructed the experience, my strongest memory was the feeling of dogged tiredness. Over the previous month I had gone nonstop, speaking to audiences totaling more than ninety-five thousand. I was physically worn out. Was that a factor?

From the Rotary Club I went to the Wayne County Vocational Center to address the entire student body. That was a struggle, too, because my mind was on the twelve-year-old boy who had taken his life. While I spoke, our representative continued to search for more information. He spoke with James Robertson, the Creston Junior High principal. Mr. Robertson provided the information about Dana's father's suicide, his mother's death, and his numerous threats. Unfortunately, the same information was not released to the media.

One local reporter seized the opportunity to write a sizzling story, not bothering to examine all the data. His biased article depicted Dana as a normal American boy from a traditional family who heard an address on suicide and two hours later killed himself. Nothing was mentioned of the father's suicide nor the fact that Dana had received psychiatric care due to his suicidal tendencies. The article, placed prominently on page one, blared the headline: "Boy Takes Life After Program on Suicide."

I was upset by the malicious implication of the news report, but my deeper concern was for Dana Golub, a boy I never knew. Lying in my bed that night, I wept for Dana. Again the thoughts plagued me: *What if? What if I had hung around afterward like I normally do? What if he had stopped to talk to me? What if I had waited just five minutes? Maybe if I had lingered at the buses that little boy would have come up to talk with me.* As far as I knew, Dana may have brushed right by my side. But there was no solace.

Continuing to race recklessly from one thought to another, my mind went back to San Diego where I had spoken just three weeks earlier. The experience in one high school came back as if I were actually reliving it. I could see them again: twelve hundred students in a typical gym. Every type, every look was represented. Punk. New wave. Freak. There were even some straights.

Before walking into that place, I had been warned that "these kids are a bit unruly." I knew what that meant. I had heard such feeble explanations before. They were telling me: Be prepared for severe disorder. I saw some kids outside the gym having what amounted to an impromptu party. "Jam boxes" were pumping out a heavy rock sound as a few kids danced to the pulsation. We had generated a lot of media attention, and several television crews were there to capture footage for their evening news.

As I began to speak, I was not about to be intimidated. I took the wireless mike in hand and walked to the edge of the platform. Staring at them in my most penetrating manner, I grabbed their attention with the forceful reality of my message. To the faculty's disbelief, there was total quiet. The kids were tuned in to what I was saying. When I finished, they left in a somber attitude. A few were weeping. One boy came to me afterward and confessed to heavy involvement in the drug scene. He was snorting coke like a fiend and was even selling the stuff. He wanted help.

A school counselor who attended the assembly felt I was too direct. He contacted some other high

131

schools where I was scheduled to speak. His insider's advice: You'd better have a psychologist present when Jerry Johnston speaks because he is emotionally jarring. Because of his slander, three schools canceled. None bothered to check out the facts. The *San Diego Tribune* addressed the matter in two articles. The DJ's on a top local rock station ridiculed the school officials who were, in their opinion, afraid of confronting teenagers.

When asked by members of the media, "Don't you think your presentation is too overwhelming for the mind of a teenager?" I answered, "Are you kidding? You're being naive and gullible. The difference between you and me is that you don't know what kids do at the Friday and Saturday night parties. I do. Realizing that—realizing those powerful influences—my presentation is not too much."

My answer did not satisfy them.

Back in Wooster, there in the quietness of that darkened hotel room, I thought again about Dana.

The next morning I was passing through the Cleveland Airport on my way to catch a flight to Richmond, Virginia. I was scheduled to speak to three thousand teenagers at an amusement park. Glancing at a newsstand, I was startled to see my picture on the front page of the *Akron-Beacon Journal*. It carried a story on the Golub incident. Changing planes in Baltimore an hour later, I picked up another newspaper. There was a story about me in that one, too! The Associated Press had picked up the biased article first published in Ohio, so all the affiliates were running it. Even the *Kansas City Times*, my hometown newspaper, ran a lengthy front-page article.

The injustice of it all staggered me. No one had truly checked out the facts. A case was built against me because of one reporter's ill-conceived article. I decided to set the record straight. In the numerous interviews that followed in the wake of Dana's death, I explained the predisposition to suicide. I clarified the details, showing that he was not the typical American kid. His was a severely messed-up life, and his own father had set a deadly example.

I commented to some reporters that I found it curious that nothing had ever been made of Ozzy Osbourne's hit song, "Suicide Solution." That song can, in fact, instill the thought of suicide, but who has attacked it? How strange that a bizarre character like Osbourne can profit from obscene suggestiveness. Then when I speak frankly to sophisticated high-school kids, some well-meaning professionals act as if I'm dealing with toddlers who need to be protected from reality.

A few weeks after the tragic events in Ohio, I was in Oklahoma City. While speaking to a large gathering, I noticed a reporter furiously taking notes. She came to me afterward, a look of surprised pleasure in her face. "Mr. Johnston," she said, "this isn't anything like what I thought it would be." Intrigued, I asked, "What are you talking about?" She smiled wryly and said, "We got a call from a reporter in Ohio who said you distribute a handbook on how to kill yourself."

I have come to expect opposition to my message, but I know it won't come from teenagers. They have never rejected what I have to say. Inevitably, the detractors are those who fail to recognize that we must talk about suicide if we are to prevent it. We must draw into the open those troubled teenagers who would talk about their anguish if someone would listen.

13

Myths about Suicide

Before you finish reading this chapter, several teen-agers will try to kill themselves. One may succeed, thereby becoming another grisly statistic. The death will make news for a day, then be forgotten by the public. But family, friends, and acquaintances will be left groping through a dense fog of uncertainty. They will wonder, evaluate, and ask time and again, "Why suicide?" The doubts will lead to speculation, and the speculation will lead to some wrong conclusions. I say this with certainty because I've seen it happen so frequently. Misconceptions about suicide are prevalent.

Many people are hesitant to even discuss the subject of suicide. That attitude in itself indicates an unhealthy fear. Suicide is such a no-no topic in our society that many—perhaps thousands—of suicidal deaths are reported instead as accidents. You, too, probably have some false ideas about suicide. I know I did. So, once and for all, let's set the record straight on several key points. Let's dispel some commonly held myths about suicide.

Myth No. 1: People who talk about suicide don't commit suicide. Wrong. Dead wrong. Dr. Edwin Shneidman, the country's leading suicide expert, blasts this idea. He says, "The notion that people who talk about suicide don't do it is the most dangerous myth in the world. Four out of five suicides have made previous attempts and in every single instance the person gives clues, warning signals, that he is about to do it."[1]

What if a suicidal person dares to talk to you about self-destructive thoughts? How will you respond? Many people, out of fear and ignorance, refuse to get involved. They think, wrongly, that discussing suicide with the suicidal person will risk heightening the danger. Not so. By expressing those morbid thoughts, the suicidal person is saying, "Help me! I'm trying to get a handle on this!"

Myth No. 2: Suicides usually happen without warning. No, suicides do not occur unpredictably. They are more often than not the result of long-term inner struggle that is expressed outwardly in some clearly recognizable actions and attitudes.

This myth is so desperately untrue that I devote an entire chapter to it. There is almost always a clue, usually several, that a person is suicidal. The next chapter, "Deadly Giveaways," thoroughly examines the warning signs.

Myth No. 3: Suicidal people can't be talked out of it if they are really intent on dying. I quote again from Dr. Shneidman:

Nonsense! [A suicidal person] is in a state of confusion and irrational thinking; he wants to continue his life but can't see the way. We find so frequently that lethal drives last just a short time so that if you

135

can get him through the period of severe stress, his entire outlook can change and the very next day he may no longer be the slightest bit suicidal.[2]

Nearly every suicidal person is torn between living and dying to such an extent that one authority says "the leap off a building may be the tragic result of a 51 to 49 internal vote."[3] For concerned friends, this wavering between the two sides is an opportunity to speak up and reach out.

Myth No. 4: An individual's improvement following a suicidal crisis means the suicide risk is over. Paul tried to hang himself because, as he put it in a terse note to his parents,

Nobody loves me. Nobody really talks to me. They just throw words at me.

Paul survived, however, and he seemed to be making improvement. "I thought he had solved his problem," said his father. But Paul made a second attempt four months after the first. Help arrived too late. His final note read,

Nobody listens. They say "How are you?" and that's about as far as it goes. I don't want to live in a world where it hurts so bad inside all the time.

Paul's case, unfortunately, is tragically typical. The person most likely to complete a suicide is one who failed in a previous attempt. Of all the signs, this one is the most foreboding. The parent's or friend's role in this circumstance is to act, not assume. Saying "I thought he was getting better" won't bring the person back. After a failed attempt, it is imperative to show you care by spending time daily with the person, talking, doing things together, enjoying life.

Myth No. 5: Suicide strikes more often among the rich. I like what N. L. Farberow says about this:

"Suicide is neither the rich man's disease nor the poor man's curse."[4] In fact, suicide is very democratic and includes a proportionate number of victims from all levels of society. Another study says that "the average person who commits suicide is close to the average person."[5]

Myth No. 6: Suicide is hereditary; it runs in families. There is absolutely no evidence to suggest that suicidal tendencies are hereditary. But there is unquestionably a powerfully negative influence on surviving families when a suicide occurs. One psychiatrist calls it survivor guilt—a curious belief that the "wrong person" died. A confused teenager told me, "My father was such a good man. He never hurt anybody and worked so hard for the family. Look at me. I'm a mess, and I keep screwing up in everything I do. Why am I the one still alive?"

When a family member takes his or her own life, it can prompt suicidal thoughts and even a suicide attempt among the survivors. This is especially true of a person already deeply troubled. But none of this has a thing to do with genetic factors. No one is doomed to act a certain way or destined to end it all because a family member made a fateful decision. I firmly believe that the suicide of Dana Golub's father was an impetus in Dana's death, but it didn't have to be that way.

Myth No. 7: Someone who commits suicide is mentally ill. Marcia attempted suicide when she was fifteen and again at seventeen. In her own words,

> The agony and the confusion at the time seemed permanent. My main concern was that if the situation I was in was going to be permanent, I wanted no part of it. That death would be permanent was of no consideration to me. There is a great feeling of being hopeless and lost and your self-image is in pretty bad shape when you're thinking about suicide.

Marcia, I'm convinced, is not mentally ill. She is quite normal and, thankfully, quite alive today. But she does illustrate the severity of adjustment during the teenage years. Like the butterfly freeing itself from the cocoon, the teenager must stretch new emotional muscles before finally breaking away. It's a wonderful, difficult time, and there are many obstacles along the way. Kids tell me about their pain, their feelings of rejection, and the ugly suspicion that no one really cares. But they aren't insane.

Some very bright young people take their own lives because they no longer want to mask the secret torment that lurks inside. A prominent medical journal recently reported its finding that 12 percent of grade-school children, age six to twelve years, have had suicidal ideas or made suicidal threats. Are these children crazy? No. Are they vulnerable? You'd better believe they are.

Myth No. 8: Only certain people are the suicidal type. There's no such thing as a suicidal personality type. This menace touches every point in a cross section of society and is not limited to certain individuals with a certain makeup. However, I would be careful to emphasize that some people are greater risks than others; those who have attempted suicide before; recently bereaved persons; the seriously ill; alcoholics and drug abusers.

Myth No. 9: The most suicides are committed by older people with just a few years to live. False. Persons over fifty are, statistically, less likely to take their lives. The most endangered group are those in the fifteen to twenty-four age bracket.

Myth No. 10: Women threaten suicide, but men carry it out. This myth comes from a misinterpreted fact. Three times as many men as women commit suicide, but three times as many women as men attempt it. The explanation for this phenomenon lies in the suicide method. Women use less violent means such as pills or poison, increasing the chance of rescue. Men are more likely to kill themselves violently with a gun, a knife, or a rope.

Myth No. 11: Talking about suicide causes suicide by planting the idea in a person's head. Some critics claim that I inadvertently encourage teenagers to commit suicide. I think just the opposite is true. You see, I know many teens are already thinking about suicide, and they are often convinced no one has ever felt the way they feel. By talking about suicide and by identifying the feelings they are experiencing, we are bringing everything out into the open. Just knowing that others are struggling, too, helps immeasurably in a teenager's ability to cope.

No, talking about suicide will not cause suicide. But failing to talk about it may have disastrous consequences.

14

Deadly Giveaways

"I can't believe it. She just wasn't the kind of person you'd expect to commit suicide. There weren't any signs at all."

I've heard comments like this many times from many people across America. There was no indication of anything wrong, they say. No clue as to a deep need. No sign of a serious problem. But, I must confess, I always raise my eyebrows in disbelief because seldom does a teenager commit suicide without giving some warning. My extensive research has borne this out, and my conversations with many who have attempted suicide reinforce this conviction. A spokesperson for the Suicide and Crisis Center in Dallas says 80 percent of teenagers who commit suicide have given one or more signs of their intention beforehand.[1]

There *are* warning signs—deadly giveaways that say a teenager is potentially suicidal. Knowing them can help prevent a tragedy. But keep in mind that there is not one exclusive type of suicidal person, and the same warning sign will be expressed differently by different individuals. Some signs relate to what a person does, others to what a person doesn't do.

1. *Withdrawal—the teen who pulls away.* To a certain extent, withdrawal is natural and good during the teenage years. Developing healthy independence equips a teen for successful adulthood. But when withdrawal is severe, when there is an obvious pulling away and into a shell, watch out.

Daily sensitivity is the key to recognizing negative withdrawal. Unfortunately, our frenetic American lifestyle often desensitizes us. Without knowing it, we can find ourselves more interested in the Cosbys than in our own family. One counselor points out that "in some families where a very hectic, busy pace is kept and family members do not give each other much attention, withdrawal may not be noticed. In fact, in some families the withdrawal may even be welcomed."[2]

Unwillingness to communicate is perhaps the most common form of withdrawal, but there are other telltale indicators. Failing grades can express a withdrawal from school. Rejection of normally pleasurable activities such as sports or hobbies may suggest a self-punishing type of withdrawal. An incessant desire to be alone can also spell a disaster in the making.

2. *Moodiness—the teen who's up and down.* Everyone is moody from time to time. We're all influenced by the weather, our health, our circumstances. Teenagers are no different. But when there are wide shifts, up one day and on the bottom the next, there is cause for alarm. One expert observes that "sudden, inexplicable euphoria or whirlwind activity after a spell of gloom" means danger.

There is ample evidence to conclude that many teens have ridden an emotional roller coaster to death.

Moodiness is closely associated with the next two warning signs.

3. *Depression—the teen who holds in*. Depression is a highly individualized experience. Some teenagers, when they are depressed, become very sullen and totally wrapped up in themselves. Others camouflage their feelings so well that no one is aware anything is happening. In such cases, the only way to find out is by somehow getting the person to talk.

Understanding how depression develops can be beneficial, too. Dr. Tim LaHaye theorizes that it nearly always is the result of anger combined with self-pity. The anger may be due to a failure, an unrealized expectation, or a personal loss. As the emotions focus on whatever prompted the anger, feelings of self-pity follow.[3]

Self-pity can give way to suicidal thoughts: *Nobody understands what I'm going through. There's no way I can get out of this situation.*

4. *Aggression—the teen who lashes out*. Many suicide attempts are preceded by violent outbursts—fights, threats, cruel insults, even destruction of property. Frequently, acts of this nature are cries for help. But this kind of aggressive behavior, though usually out of character, often achieves the opposite result: rejection rather than consideration. The teenager who wanted to be noticed is condemned instead.

A less-obvious form of presuicidal aggression is risk-taking. This could include recklessness with vehicles or participation in dangerous activities. An eighteen year old boasted that a death wish motivated him to take up skydiving and wing walking on airplanes. In counseling it was discovered that he was trying to get the attention of his father who ignored him.

5. *Alcohol and drug abuse—the teen who turns on*. Alcohol and drugs are always an escape, but especially for the teenager with life-ending thoughts. Sudden indulgence by a young person who hadn't previously gotten drunk or done drugs is a definite red flag.

6. *Sexual activity—the teen who lets go*. Inappropriate sexual behavior sometimes reflects a desperate desire to relieve depression. By letting go completely with another person, the depressed teenager thinks satisfaction can finally be achieved. When there is no lasting satisfaction, suicidal thoughts can and often do intensify.

7. *Eating disorders—the teen who punishes self. Anorexia* and *bulimia* are words now well-known by most Americans. These frightful diseases have a strong connection to self-destructive thoughts and should always be considered potentially suicidal. Concerned friends and family members should watch for drastic weight loss. The celebrated case of pop singer Karen Carpenter, who died of an anorexia-induced heart attack, is a potent example of the risk. Hers was an unintentional suicide.

8. *Gift giving—the teen who gives up and gives away*. Some teenagers who plan to take their lives will give away prized possessions to close friends or to others they wish were close friends. Suicide experts say this is an ominous action, a silver cloud with a very dark lining. It should prompt serious, concerned questioning.

9. *Trauma—the teen who's been hit hard*. Each person has an emotional threshold, an internal breaking point. A major traumatic event or series of circumstances can drive a teenager closer and closer to that edge. A family move to another community or city can seem like the end of the world to

a young person who has built strong ties and sunk deep roots. The trauma of a divorce, a death, an accident—any such experience can hit a teenager hard, leaving the young person stunned with thoughts of suicide running through the mind.

10. *Personality change—the teen who's not the same*. Abrupt reversal is the thing to watch for. When a usually introverted person suddenly begins to act like an unbridled extrovert, joking and carrying on, it's not a laughing matter. Conversely, this holds true as well when the gregarious person becomes a silent loner. Personality change is also expressed in a lessened energy level, neglect of responsibility, or an I-don't-care attitude toward personal appearance.

11. *Threat—the teen who speaks out*. Any comment regarding the desire to die should be taken seriously. Some of the most common threats are "I wish I'd never been born" or "You're going to be sorry when I'm gone" or "I want to go to sleep and never wake up." These should be interpreted as seriously as "I'm going to kill myself."

As I've mentioned repeatedly, diligently watch for these signs. Don't feel helpless, because you're not. You can help a suicidal person. You must communicate with the person, asking questions to probe the troubled individual's conscience. You must empathize, not being judgmental or harsh, but not being overly sympathetic either. And you must act. In the following pages I'll give more specific guidelines on what you can do.

15

The Hurt Never Goes Away

A Plea to Parents

A friend of mine was cutting paper on a large trimmer when his hand slipped into the blade's path. In an instant, the edge of his index finger was severed. Though in moderate shock, he managed to wrap a handkerchief around the wound and hold it there tightly all the way to the hospital. Since the index finger is amazingly sensitive, he was in agony. After treatment in the emergency room, he was released. Recuperation wasn't easy. For several days he had to keep his injured hand elevated at all times to restrict the flow of blood and lessen the pain. He had to take strong medication. And still the finger throbbed incessantly, sometimes feeling as if it were a thermometer about to explode. In subsequent weeks he made eight visits to a plastic surgeon for reconstructive treatment.

Today, my friend's finger looks perfectly normal. It is not deformed in any manner. But he tells me that because of nerve damage, it always has a tingling sensation. The initial pain is gone, but there is a constant reminder of that one traumatic moment when part of him was cut off.

Though it may at first seem strange, I see in my friend's experience a remarkable parallel to the process a family goes through when one of its members commits suicide. Initially, there is indescribable anguish, deep beyond imagination. Then there is a slow, difficult healing period. Various "medicines" must be taken to endure the trauma. The help of others is essential as reconstruction continues, if ever so tediously. Finally, everything appears to be back to normal, at least to outsiders. But it isn't. It never is, nor can it ever be. When there is emotional nerve damage, the tingling reminder of past hurt is always there.

In the hundreds of opportunities I've had to counsel suicidal teenagers, I tell them: "Think about the damage you're going to cause. You'll leave behind loved ones riddled with guilt, overcome with despairing thoughts, puzzled over questions never to be answered." I put it bluntly: "The ones you leave behind will never be the same again. Never!" And I add: "They will blame themselves for your self-centered act of final defiance. What's more, if you kill yourself, you may cause a brother or sister or friend to take the same foolish step."

When I spoke to the student body of Liberty Junior High School in Liberty, Missouri, there was understandably rapt attention. Four teenagers in that typically midwestern suburb of Kansas City had committed suicide within months of each other. The entire community was asking, Why is this happening to us, to our children? During my lecture, I was unaware that in the audience sat the grieving mother of a fifteen-year-old boy who had taken his own life. He was the second in that fateful string of four senseless deaths. After my address that afternoon, I met Barbara Stoufer and learned

146

about the devastating loss of her son, Aaron. Later, in the living room of the Stoufers' home, I heard the grim details. So relevant and compelling is the story, I asked permission to share it in the pages of this book. Mr. and Mrs. Stoufer graciously agreed to my request.

Bear in mind that Aaron Stoufer lived in a balanced, happy home. He did not use drugs or alcohol. Never did he suggest to anyone that he might take his own life. Yet Aaron's death was part of that cluster of four teen suicides in Liberty.

Dennis Stoufer, Aaron's father, recalls:

"The morning of April 3, 1984, was the last time I saw Aaron alive. Minutes before he boarded the bus about 7:00, he and I joked and teased each other. He poked me in the side with his elbow and smirked, 'Fat man, leave me alone.' It was his way of kidding me for being a little overweight. I yelled, 'Have a good day,' as Aaron left for school. Moments later I headed East on a marketing trip for my company.

"I stopped at Terre Haute, Indiana, about four hundred miles away. While unpacking my business supplies in the hotel room, the phone rang. Dr. Rogers, my neighbor, was on the other end. 'Dennis,' he said sternly, 'there's been a shooting.' I was still taking in the words when he added, 'Barbara, Mary, and Travis are fine. But Aaron's dead.' My mind went blank, and my emotions froze as I heard myself mumble, 'Oh, no.' My body became instantly numb. Somehow I managed to ask, 'Where's Barbara?' She came on the line. 'Dennis, come home. I need you,' she said in a hollow, desperate voice. After that, Dr. Rogers said something else, but I don't remember what. But I did grasp the fact that Aaron had shot himself.

"Across Interstate 70 on the way home, I cried almost continually. I kept asking God why He would allow something like this to happen. I searched my heart, asking, What did I do wrong? How did I fail Aaron?

"Arriving about 2:00 in the morning, I let myself into the house and went into Aaron's bedroom, where he had killed himself. I fell down on my knees at the edge of the bed and wept bitterly. I prayed for courage, for peace, for help. Both my mind and body were in shock.

"Barb was at a neighbor's house down the street. I went down to see how she was taking everything. Our two other children, seven-year-old Mary and four-year-old Travis, had been taken to stay with other friends nearby. I phoned to see how they were. Then determining it would be better for Barb to stay where she was, I returned to the house. Another friend came with me and stayed for the next few hours.

"I couldn't sleep. In my anxiety I went fifty-four hours without any rest. Finally, in my zombielike state, exhaustion overtook me.

"Confusion swirled in my mind. I recall thinking, *Two plus two just don't add up to four any more*. I couldn't make normal decisions. Even deciding what to eat for breakfast seemed an impossibility.

"Gradually, I began to move out of the shock. But I couldn't understand why Aaron didn't reach out to us. Then I started to blame myself again. At the same time I tried to compose myself so that I could think about all sorts of practical questions: What was going to happen to Mary and Travis? What about funeral arrangements? Who should tell Aaron's close friends? I really didn't want to cope with any of those things, but I knew it had to be done.

"Hundreds of times since then I have asked, What if? What if I had tried to talk to him more? What if I had not driven away that morning? A year after Aaron's death I saw the movie *Back to the Future* and broke into tears because, unlike the people in the film, I couldn't go back and relive things and change the outcome.

"Even Travis and Mary have asked, 'Didn't Aaron like us enough?' 'Was he mad at us?' 'Did Aaron hate us?' 'Did he kill himself because of us?'

"'No, of course, not,' we would say, then remind them of the many times when Aaron would take them out to play in the backyard or the neighborhood.

"Aaron didn't talk to his best friends about taking his life, and apparently he didn't even hint at the possibility. I find myself going back to his childhood, wondering what I did wrong or where I failed. Even now, two years later, I'm still reviewing the past. I've retrieved from memory all the times I grounded him or spanked him for things I didn't approve of. I've asked, Did I somehow provoke it—the thought of killing himself?

"I remember one incident when Aaron was four. He darted across the street, and I had to run after him. It frightened me so much, I whipped his bottom fifteen or twenty times. He went inside, sobbing his little eyes out. I have wondered if that was physical abuse or if I punished him too hard. The memory troubles me. Yet, about a year before his death, I overheard Aaron recount the whole episode to a friend. He said, 'Yeah, my dad whipped my butt to show me he didn't want me to get injured out in the street.' I realize, with great pain, that I will never know what was really in his mind and how that experience really affected him.

"As a surviving father, I am deeply concerned about teenagers who are at crisis points and thinking about suicide. I urge them, I beg them, to give their parents a chance. So often, a teenager will think that mom and/or dad don't understand. I remember feeling that very way when I was growing up. But mom and dad often do understand. Try, just try to talk to them. Suicide is a one-time, one-sided statement, but the trauma inflicted upon those left behind is felt time and time again.

"I think about Aaron every day. On some occasions, like his birthday, the thoughts of him are so overpowering. I even find myself counting days since his death. For example, I know that New Year's Eve 1987 is 1,002 days after Aaron died.

"For the rest of my life, I never want a day to go by that Aaron isn't a part of it. I want the memory of him to create in me an ever-deepening awareness of life's preciousness. I want it to make me kinder, more loving, more sensitive to my other children. I want his death to have an enduring significance."

The words of Dennis Stoufer grip my heart as if it were placed in a vise. Each thought he shares turns that vise a notch tighter. Pressed and pressured, I am moved to examine painstakingly my relationship with my own children. As a father, I can identify with Dennis, and I can learn from his excruciating experience. I know that is what he desires.

Aaron Stoufer also left behind a heartbroken mother. Listen now to her words:

"It started out like a typical school morning. Everyone was rushing around, getting ready, eating breakfast. Aaron finally made it out the door and headed for his bus stop. He came home happy that afternoon about 3:15, joking around the way he often did. A few minutes later he overheard a conversation about my getting a baby-sitter for the next night. That upset him. He reminded me that he was fifteen and a responsible person.

"'You don't trust me anymore,' he said. 'Is that it?'

"'Aaron,' I replied, 'we can talk about that later.' I

was in a hurry because I had some errands to run, and I wanted to get back before dark. My answer wasn't unusual because at night we regularly had discussions.

"Many times we would sit and talk after I put the two younger ones to bed. Our real feelings would then come out. Aaron would tell me things he wouldn't share with his father. He talked about his girlfriends, about the things they would say, and I think he felt hesitant to relate that to Dennis. Especially when his father was on the road, Aaron and I would talk in the evenings. So, he understood when I said we'd talk about it later. But I didn't get that time with him, and he never gave me a chance to explain.

"I didn't realize how upset Aaron was. I thought it was just a disagreement, or a little disappointment, like the difference of opinion when I'd want him to wear a different shirt to school. That day, though, he became more quiet and wasn't joking as much as he normally did. Looking back, I believe his feelings about the situation worsened. When we came back from the errands about 5:00, Aaron went to his room.

"A short time later, I was startled by banging and pounding noises from Aaron's room. In a violent emotional outburst he was destroying everything he could get his hands on, smashing objects against the wall, tearing shelves down, acting wildly. He had never done anything like that before.

"'Stop it, Aaron!' I yelled. I raced into his room and yelled again. He kept throwing things. I grabbed his shoulder and shook him. 'Do you hear me?' He nodded and looked away.

"'Clean this up. I'm very upset that you've broken some very valuable things.' I walked out of the room and headed for the bathroom where the other children were getting cleaned up. It was nearly six

151

o'clock. Behind me, Aaron evidently left his room and went into our bedroom.

"In our bedroom we kept a .22 Magnum. It was a weapon Aaron had fired numerous times. He was an excellent marksman and knew the damage a bullet could do. Aaron went straight to that gun. I heard a terrible sound, like the popping of a loud balloon.

"When I heard the shot, I turned and raced back into the bedroom. The strangest feeling came over me. I had heard people talk about the angel of death, and that day I sensed his presence. Something was definitely there. As soon as I saw Aaron's body, I turned around. Because of the noise, the other children had followed me.

"'What happened, Mama?'

"'Just—just go back to the bathroom. I'll be there in a minute.'

"'What was that awful noise?' Mary asked.

"'Just go back. I'll be right there.' I felt a terrible surge of panic within me, a dreadful numbness. Without any conscious thought I ran across the street to the Rogers' house. Dr. Rogers is a medical doctor, so I desperately needed his help. I knocked so hard the door flew open by itself. Dr. Rogers was at home. I blurted out what had happened, and he raced ahead of me across the street.

"'Call 911—the emergency number!' he shouted. I phoned, and the paramedic unit arrived within minutes. By then, Travis and Mary were crying, not understanding what was going on but sensing that things weren't right. I wanted to calm them down and comfort them, but I couldn't even do anything for myself at the time.

"I went into shock, overcome with disbelief. Everything seemed so unreal. I started calling my church friends. 'I need you. I need you now,' I kept saying over and over to them. 'Pray, please pray like you've never prayed before.' I groaned out repeatedly, 'God, help us, help us get through this.'

"The full brunt of tragedy hit me when the doctor came out of the bedroom. He looked directly at me and said, 'Aaron is dead.' Dr. Rogers is a good friend, and he'd always been straightforward with us. A wave of weakness engulfed me, and I started to fall. Dr. Rogers grabbed me. Irrationally, I struck out at him. 'No! No!' I cried.

"Later I went to a neighbor's house and did get a little sleep. I woke up about 5:00 in the morning and went back up to the house and into the bedroom. I knelt down and prayed, pleading with God to help us through this. After a long time in the bedroom, I did feel more peaceful. That was the beginning of God's peace filling the void in my heart left by Aaron's death.

"We have what I always considered a basically good family life, and never did I imagine anything like this happening to us. And for it to come so suddenly, without any warning.

"Some dear friends took care of Travis and Mary and gave them a lot of attention, helping in those crucial days. About two months later, Mary started to have seizures. The doctor thought it was due to stress. She's still on daily medication. Shortly after Aaron's death, Dennis's mother died. Then my grandfather died. To Mary, it seemed that everybody was dying around her. We learned much later on that she had overheard a police officer saying that there had possibly been a murder. She tortured herself, wondering if someone had been in the house or if I had shot her brother.

"It was several weeks before Mary started talking about Aaron's death. That's when I learned that she and Travis had gone in and seen their brother's body when I ran across the street. It was very difficult for her, but she managed to relate everything that had happened that night. There was an obvious relief, but she cried long and hard. Still, the hurt was there, and for weeks afterward Mary would start crying for no apparent reason. Occasionally, she even had nightmares.

"Another boy in Liberty had taken his life, and I had talked with Aaron about it. I now think Aaron may have toyed with the idea of suicide after that incident. I had talked with him the night of the other boy's death.

"'Did you know the boy?'

"'Yes.'

"'How well?'

"'Kinda good, but not like a friend.' Then he said it was a bad thing, and he didn't want to talk about it anymore.

"The day of Aaron's death, he had seemingly had a good day, according to his teachers, his girlfriend, and his schoolmates. And, ordinarily, when he got into an argument with me, he'd go outside and work it off or kick a soccer ball around the yard. He'd vent his frustration on something else. There was just nothing for us to suspect his getting mad enough to do something so severe. We never saw him so charged up emotionally as he was that night.

"The hurt never goes away. You start learning to live with it and accept that it's going to be there the rest of your life. But still it hurts. Ours is definitely a labored existence, though I'm better now than a year ago.

"After Aaron died, I considered suicide myself. *Why not?* I thought, in my depression and confusion. Quite often I slept a lot or at least tried to. That was a hardship on the two little ones because they were not used to my new behavior. I had always gotten up and fixed their breakfast. I had always washed their clothes, and the house was kept clean. All of that changed for a while. It was hard to do housework, hard to cook, hard to do anything.

"Somehow I made it, finally deciding I couldn't hurt any worse. I had such a void in my life because Aaron and I were close. Or so I thought. But were we, really? Thoughts like these tormented me for a long time.

"For some time friends would tell me, 'It's time to get on with your life.' But the words didn't help. In fact, they made me feel worse. Finally, though, after about a year and a half, I began to feel more energetic.

"I struggled with a few thoughts about the stigma of Aaron's death on us. But I didn't feel that I had to explain anything to anybody about what had happened.

"Some things still bother me. Like noises. Certain pops or shattering sounds cause the memories to roll back over me. It reminds me of that gun going off.

"Being a mother and losing one of your children causes such an emptiness. I learned the value of talking about it, and I was helped by those who were willing to simply listen.

"Almost every day I see Aaron's friends when they get off the bus. Sometimes they look toward the house. For them it's not the same, because Aaron's not here anymore. They still ask questions when I talk to them. 'Do you know why he did it?' or 'Could we have done something to prevent it?' Some have even said that they've come by the house in the evening and glanced up, wanting to see his image in the window of his room.

"Every day I still wonder, What if I had done something in a different way, would it have made a difference? If I had stopped and talked instead of saying we would do it later. If I had been more sensitive to his mood, or loved him more, would he have been kept from taking his own life? I don't know how to answer my own questions, yet I must live with them every day.

"Aaron brought much love and joy into our lives. I'm glad he was here for fifteen years. I want his love to live on and help me be a better mother and wife and friend. Maybe if I can use what I've learned over these difficult times, I can be a better person.

"The if's are endless, as is the hurt in not seeing his smiling face and enjoying his presence."

I am constantly asked by parents, "How can I better relate to my teenager?" The question usually reflects an attitude of frustration and fear. Frustration with the feeling that we're-not-getting-through-to-each-other and fear of driving the teen away. When there is division between parents and teens, it's a lousy life for everyone.

Here's what I suggest to concerned moms and dads:

1. *Be aware*. Know what is going on in your teenager's life. And I don't mean to be nosy about every little detail. I'm referring to the need to stay abreast of what's happening at school, in friendships, in personal projects. Of course, this demands communication with your teenager—not in a looking-down-the-nose way, but with genuine openness and interest. Make it known that you care and that you are in touch with the important details of your child's life.

Of course, awareness also means being cognizant of problems and potential problems. When you see one, deal with it wisely and patiently.

2. Be *available and accessible*. I can't tell you how many kids have come to me dismayed because they are convinced that their parents are both out of

touch and untouchable. Even though your teenager may not come to you often, he or she needs to know that the door is open. Whenever your child wants to talk, especially about some troubling matter, listen. Listen as a friend.

3. *Be accepting.* For starters, accept your teenager's dress and music. The only exceptions to this, in my opinion, are in the areas of extreme or bizarre behavior. In clothing, whatever is stylish to your teenager may not seem "normal" to you, but you should accept it. In music, the same applies. Only music that is degrading and perverse, like that I described in the chapter "Rock 'n' Role Models," should be forbidden. The rest you should willingly accept, even if you don't like it.

4. *Be active.* Do things together. Get involved in sports, hobbies, and work projects that you both enjoy. This is absolutely essential for optimum communication.

There is no formula every family can follow that guarantees success, but in most cases disaster can be averted if you follow these simple guidelines. And both you and your teenager will be richer for it.

16

Some Life and Death Lessons for Teachers

A Plea to Teachers

Patty, a high school junior with above average grades and many friends, broke up with her boyfriend. They had gone together for two years. Patty tried talking it over with her parents, but they teased her about puppy love and said she'd get over it as soon as the next boy came along.

The talk ended in a loud argument, and Patty ran into the bathroom and slammed the door. Unknown to her parents, she grabbed a bottle of prescription sleeping pills and a bottle of pain killers. Minutes later she raced from the house.

Patty drove to the other side of town, an area where the family had once lived. She bought a six-pack of colas, parked outside the grammar school she had once attended, and swallowed all the pills.

As she waited for the pills to take effect, she thought about her days in grammar school. She remembered one teacher, Mrs. Blanchard, who had been kind and friendly. Patty started the car and drove to a public phone. The operator helped her get Mrs. Blanchard's number.

"This is Patty and I've just overdosed and I'm going to die. I just wanted to thank you for everything you did for me when I was in your class."

Mrs. Blanchard made Patty tell her where she was, called the hospital for an ambulance, and met Patty as the paramedics wheeled her into the emergency room.

That teacher saved Patty's life.

We need more teachers like Mrs. Blanchard. Unfortunately, some teachers regard their profession as only a job, and they make little attempt to relate to their students on a personal level.

And other teachers see only the problems and complications of young people and give up. Some commonly heard comments are "You can never curb the problem, so why try?" "Drugs have been here ever since I had a job, and they'll always be here." "Kids are going to end up blowing themselves away because they're in such horrible home environments, and we can't do anything to change that."

I've been traveling across America, talking in schools and in conferences with educators, teachers, principals, school administrators, and students. Some of them care—and they care a whole lot. Others care, but they don't seem to know how to help.

Because of their positions, teachers can do much to help. A lot of Pattys are out there, wanting to believe in an adult, wanting just one teacher to relate to. Here are twelve tips for teachers who want to help.

1. *Make yourself available.* Be sensitive to your students' moods and needs. Express frequently your desire to get to know them one-on-one—but not on the basis of your desire to counsel with them. If teenagers know you care about them, you won't have to offer to listen to their problems. They'll come to you because you care.

159

Here is a letter from a high school boy in St. Louis, Missouri, where I spoke:

> Hi, the reason of this letter is because I'm a druggie and I was at Desoto High School when you came there to talk. I've got to get some help because I think I should not live in this world any more. I've got to have pot or some other drugs before I go to bed. Please help me. I'm crying out for help. I may not live any more.

2. Be faithful to your students. Hold in confidence the things said in confidence. Too often when I stand before school audiences and say "Talk to your teacher or counselor," the one thousand or more kids snicker and laugh. To them, the last person they would ever think of going to and talking to is a teacher or a counselor. They have some good reasons for that.

They've been betrayed in the past. If not by you, by someone else in the profession. They went to counselors or teachers and told them about their problems. Those professionals went directly to their parents and repeated what they learned. Or they gossiped to other teachers and leaked the information to other students or to brothers or sisters.

Unless it becomes a matter of life and death, it is not professionally ethical to divulge counseling information, whether or not students preface the information with the statement, "I don't want anyone to know." Joan wrote me a letter that illustrates this point:

> I feel so alone and I feel like you're the only one in the whole world who I can talk to.
> I don't really have any real close friends anymore, but recently I met this group of girls who are into all kinds of drugs. And I found myself being offered drugs: pot, speed, and I accepted. And now I'm

afraid. I am afraid of getting into drugs but I'm also afraid that if I say no they won't want to be friends and then I'd be back where I was before—alone.

I just don't know what to do anymore. The counselor I'm going to now tells my parents everything, even if I ask her not to. I don't need someone to run to my parents every time I tell them something. So it always ends up that I don't tell her anything any more.

Lately I've been thinking about hanging myself. I don't want to but I can't go on like this anymore . . .

3. *Move to your students' level. Find out what's going on in the world of young people.* Too often teenagers are turned off by teachers and counselors whom they automatically stereotype as busy people who care little about students.

Some students feel teachers act as if they couldn't identify with teenagers who want to drink, do drugs, or have sex—activities that teens call fun today and that almost everybody does. A part of all of us wants to do the same things, and we need to face these facts. But students "know" when they approach the ultra-straight and ultra-square that those teachers would never have any desire to do such things.

Christy wrote me this sad note and enclosed a poem:

I wrote this just before my last suicide attempt. This is how I felt. I don't know if I feel this way now. I'm just confused.

> I thought there was such a thing as love
> Though now I know I'm wrong.
> I'll never find someone to love
> Anyone like me.
> So now I go and leave this world
> And into a deep sleep stay.
> Please do not cry or shed

Even one lonely tear.
Just look in your heart.
I will always be there.

4. *Talk without giving orders.* Teenagers don't want to be preached at when they have problems. They want someone to listen. Simply by listening and showing that you understand, you can help them get over many of their problems.

By listening you'll help teenagers face the problems of despair, personal dilemma, drugs, alcohol, or whatever their problems may be.

It's probably a waste of time writing to you because (1) you're just too darn busy to read letters from unimportant people, (2) you have thousands of letters like this one and (3) I'm not special. For example, I'm not dying or contributing one million dollars . . . Sorry about that.

I've listened to you in person, and I've listened to your tapes. And quite frankly, I like you, sir. But I wonder about things. Are you sincere? Do you speak the truth? Do you *really* care about people? Will I ever have the chance of hearing you speak again? Questions such as these.

I'd like to say briefly that the last time I entrusted personal problems to [an adult] that very [person turned] out to be taking drugs—such as cocaine! . . . I can't tell you how terribly betrayed I felt. I pray that you are different because we teens need someone we can really trust.

Love and respect,
Kelly

5. *Disseminate effective material.* Avoid material written for those with doctoral degrees or for those with ten-dollar-a-word vocabularies. Naturally, materials must be accurate and certain information of value, but teenagers must be able to relate to them.

Here is an unsigned letter I received from a teenage boy. His first sentence apparently refers to the lecture I gave at his school.

> I thought it was dumb because people who can't handle drugs should not try it. I can handle it. The only reason I am still alive is because of pot, skiing, and girls. But . . . if you had people around you like me, you would do drugs, too.

6. Be alert. Look for trouble. Teachers and other school workers are usually the first professionals to encounter suicidal children and that puts them in a position to recognize the seriousness of the emotional disturbance.

Watch for tell-tale signs such as depression—the most frequent cause of suicide. Depression is often triggered in young people by feelings of loss. Watch for other predictable circumstances such as divorce, new transfers to school, and unstable parental job situations.

Alert teachers are ready to grapple with these situations and help when students need to talk to somebody.

Here's part of a letter from a teenager who finally went to a teacher for help. She tells of her problems and then says:

> Then my sister had me over to help with her new baby and my brother-in-law molested me . . . I didn't know what to do. I just cried all night. I told my sister and they got it all straightened out. But I could not come near him at all. My parents didn't know. No one but the three of us.
>
> It kept building up inside of me. Then one night I tried to kill myself. The next day I had to talk to someone so I went to one of the teachers and got it all straightened out.

7. Feel—and let them know you feel. Young people feel loss keenly, loss of almost anything—loss of a parent, loss of success in school, loss of self-esteem or self-respect, loss of friends, loss of a football or basketball game, loss of a familiar neighborhood, even the loss of childhood.

Try to watch closely those students whom you know have experienced a definable loss—the loss of a parent through divorce or death, for instance, or the loss of the familiar because of a move. Most teenagers struggle with the loss of their security and identity as children. When this inevitable but painful loss is complicated by yet another loss, serious problems often develop.

Be especially on the alert for teens who have recently moved and are trying to fit into the school. They want to fit in, but they're not always readily accepted. Maybe they're teased, made fun of, or just left out. They'll talk about special friends they had at their old schools or about teachers they could talk to when they were upset or confused. Please don't underestimate these feelings, these losses.

8. *Be especially alert to behavioral changes.* Young people are action-oriented, and they often reveal their feelings through actions rather than words. Sudden changes in behavior can be warning signals.

Allan's records, for example, show high academic achievement through the ninth grade. Now in the tenth grade, he barely passes and frequently picks fights with other boys. Of course, the new subject matter may be too difficult. But watch that student closely. Allan may be trying to raise his self-esteem by punching out the next guy. Maybe he is trying to compensate in the physical area for failures in the academic area. If so, being punished will only further lower his self-esteem. Punishment is attention, but it's not the attention he needs. It doesn't get at what really troubles him. He may have an emotional problem at home or something serious may be going on inside Allan.

Similarly when Barbara, who has generally been well-behaved, starts to become disruptive, look beyond the symptoms. Why does she start arguments? Why has she become difficult to reason with? What has caused her hostility and lack of co-operation? Barbara may feel lousy about herself. She may feel ugly or unpopular or stupid. Maybe she feels left out or lonely. Her hostility and anger, even though lashing out, may be an expression of her desire for self-destruction. A perceptive, caring teacher may be able to help Barbara sort out her negative feelings and come to terms with the real source of her anger.

One insightful teacher said, "Disturbing behavior is not the problem. It is only a symptom of the problem."

If teachers can't help teenagers like Allan and Barbara by providing some relief from their problems and their pain, these troubled teenagers may find their own relief. They may find it in drugs, sex, alcohol, or suicide.

9. Don't become a junior psychiatrist. That's dangerous. You might open wounds you cannot close. Once you show you care, you can listen. You can probe, but don't try to solve problems by using techniques you learned from a college psychology class. Stay in your field as a teacher who wants to be a friend. Listening and caring are two unbeatable techniques you have to offer.

A junior-high student who signed himself S.O.S. wrote me a letter. He gave it to one of his teachers and asked him to pass it on. In the letter to his teacher he wrote:

P.S. Please give it to him. My life is counting on him. If he would like to get in touch with me faster, he

165

can ask my friend, Bob, in Mrs. Mitchell's home-room.

In his letter to me, S.O.S. included drawings on the envelope with a note: *Doomsday for some people and maybe me in one week.*

I just wanted to talk to you about what you were telling us Monday. I'm in the eighth grade. What I'm trying to say is that I was going to kill myself after school that day.

I thought about it now. I think I will go ahead and do it. I'm scared to do it. I never took drugs before, but I think that's what I'll use to kill myself. I thought it would help.

I had talked to my best friend about it. He said it wouldn't help. It would just make it worster. *All I want to do is talk to you about it.* But first I would get my best friend, Bob, to talk to you to make sure it is o.k. for me to talk to you. I can trust him . . .

P.S. I'll tell you why I want to kill myself.

10. *Make referrals.* If the school has a psychologist, a social worker, and/or a counselor, take advantage of their specialized skills. This doesn't mean you have to back out of the picture. You can say, "You have real problems and I wish you'd talk to Ms. Gannett, the school counselor. I'd still like to be available for you to talk to whenever you want. But your situation is beyond my depth."

If you show your willingness to be there, to be someone to talk to, and that you care, you are doing the best you can do. Don't attempt to function as a psychiatric professional.

A parent sent the following letter to her daughter's school principal following one of my talks:

The tape of that young boy's suicide frightened Gail, saddened her and gave her a lot more insight into the real, horrible, and killing world of drugs. I am thankful she was scared, I am thankful she did shed tears for this boy's agony, but the thing I am most thankful for is, because of Jerry's message, she said she had never tried drugs, and she swore she *never never* would try them.

I don't know if Gail would ever have gotten involved with drugs, but because of you and Jerry, I honestly believe that she will not be tempted to experiment—she said she will never forget the lessons taught to her Wednesday.

I thank you for being the wonderful educator that you are and I thank everyone else connected with this program.

11. *Contact parents.* While teachers need to hold matters in confidence, there are times they need to contact the parents. If you sense that a teenager is suicidal, this puts a duty on you to warn and to do anything possible to prevent that student from destroying his or her life.

Communicate with the parents confidentially. You may need to say that you think their son or daughter is suicidal. Let the parents know of your concern and the reasons for it. Alert them. Occasionally a parent will resent this, but most are appreciative. Working together, you and the parent can find a remedy.

12. *Ask help from other teachers.* Seek insight and help from other teachers who know the student. If those teachers confirm what you have observed—for example, that Barbara has suddenly become disruptive—it confirms your feelings. You know you are on to something.

Of course, what I am saying assumes that teachers have classes of manageable size. Otherwise, you are not likely to be able to provide the individual attention that enables a troubled child to be spotted.

In offering these tips, I am not trying to place guilt on teachers for not doing more. After a suicide occurs in a school or community, there is more than enough guilt to go around. You can even help there. Students will ask each other and you, "Why did we ignore Allan?" "Why were we so mean to him?" You and other teachers will ask yourselves questions such as, "Why didn't I notice he was troubled?" "Was it my fault—because I failed him on his last exam?"

You can help these people. They don't need toothy smiles and phony assurances of, "Don't worry—it wasn't your fault." Those words mean nothing. They need someone to listen and to hear them speak of their own sense of failure. And if they failed, help them to accept it. It may help if you analyze what went on, explain its complexity, and provide the guidance that will allow them to come to terms with their guilt, their sadness, and their fear.

An editorial addressed to teachers, principals, and school officials appeared in *USA Today* and says that in case of a suicide:

> . . . the principal should not wait. By the time he hears the details, the rest of the school will have heard the details, too, in 40 different versions.
>
> The principal must notify the parents. Then, he should call a school-wide assembly and explain as much as he knows. If students are let out without any explanations, they will make up their own.
>
> He should designate staff students can turn to. He should have mental health professionals there to answer questions. Ideally, teachers would already have information about suicide and depression.
>
> That evening, he should hold a community meeting for all parents and students. This will give the parents information. It will let the teen-agers have a forum for their concerns and a place to go rather

than hanging out and escalating the hysteria these situations often provoke.

The mental health professionals should be in school all day, every day, for the next three weeks. They should speak to all close friends and class-mates of the boy who committed suicide. They should target and support any who have recently ex-perienced a loss, particularly one by death.

The principal should *not* call off school so every-one can attend the funeral. Kids need to express their grief; they do not need to romanticize a mis-take.

A boy tragically made the wrong choice. This calls for sorrow, not honor. We should not make a young-ster who made a poor choice into a hero. Instead, we should applaud the wisdom of those who choose to start psychotherapy and take constructive action to deal with their concerns.[1]

17

You Can Stop a Speeding Bullet

A Plea to Friends

Susan didn't make it to school that day. While I was speaking to her classmates about the suicide crisis, she was at home, taking her own life. Susan, they tell me, was a lovely girl with many friends. How I wish she had been in that high school assembly!

Three days later I attended the funeral. Several of Susan's bereaved classmates came to me and asked, "Jerry, couldn't we have done something to help her? How could we have known this was going to happen?" In that situation I was unable to give a lengthy answer to their pleading question. But I assured them, there are things that a concerned friend can do to detect suicidal attitudes and prevent suicide attempts.

Here's what I suggest:

1. *Don't back away.* Suppose your friend starts to act strangely. You sense that some dark influence is creeping into the person's brain, and you want to back away. Please don't. When your friend has depressive or even twisted thoughts, that's the time to

make yourself more available and interested than ever.

Dee said, "I'm alive today because my best friend wouldn't leave me alone. I was going downhill, and I kept telling her to bug off, and she kept saying things like, 'Real friends don't leave when their friends are in trouble.' I really didn't want her to leave, but I didn't think anyone cared for me."

What if you don't know for sure that there's a life-threatening problem lurking inside your friend? Don't take chances! One expert counsels: "Even if you're not completely sure about the seriousness of the depression in yourself or a friend, it's better to take the necessary steps and find out you were wrong than to say nothing and find out you were right."[1]

2. *Be a detective.* I'm not suggesting that you stalk your friend or steal a glance at a personal diary. But I am saying to be on the lookout for problems or potential problems. The best way to accomplish this is by encouraging your friend to talk whenever you sense something wrong.

What can you ask? If your friend has not seemed well lately, ask something like, "You don't seem like yourself. Is there anything you'd like to talk about?" If your friend says yes and tells you about negative feelings and thoughts, don't hesitate to ask if these include thoughts of suicide. "When in doubt, check it out. If you're suspicious, ask the person directly," says family counselor Cynthia Taylor.[2]

If your friend admits to thinking about suicide, your next step is to ask, "Do you have a plan?" If the answer is affirmative, get the details. The more specific the details, the more serious the situation. More about this in a minute.

Being a good detective demands a knowledge of the suicidal warning signs. Review them periodically in the chapter, "Deadly Giveaways."

3. *Listen carefully.* Your suicidal friend must know that someone is truly willing to listen. Chances are your friend will feel that no one at home is tuned in, so you've got to show that you are. An insightful report in the *FBI Law Enforcement Bulletin* said,

> Many suicidal young people have the inability or lack of opportunity to express their unhappiness, frustration, or failure. They find that their efforts to express their feelings are either totally unacceptable to their parents, ignored, or met by defensive hostility. This response then drives the child into further isolation, reinforcing the belief of something being terribly wrong.[3]

In Omaha, Nebraska, where five students in the same high school attempted suicide in less than two weeks (three succeeded), other teenagers got concerned and got involved. A network of listeners was organized to avert more tragedy. In Plano, Texas, hit by eleven teenage suicides in just sixteen months, students set up BIONIC (Believe It Or Not I Care) and SWAT (Students Working All Together). Through these organizations, they befriended newly transferred or depressed classmates. Adults created a twenty-four-hour hotline. The payoff: No teenage suicide has been reported in Plano since May 12, 1984.[4]

As you listen, remember that your friend may be pointed or very vague. "Verbally, teenagers make direct references to killing themselves by asking, 'What would you say if I were to kill myself?' Indirectly, they might say, 'Everyone will be better off without me,' or 'You won't have to worry about me much longer.' Any reference to dying must be taken seriously."[5]

4. *Say the right things.* Remember that asking a person about suicide will not plant the idea in the mind. In fact, it says, "I've been paying attention to

you, and I see something's wrong." One author explains:

It is not unusual for teenagers to respond, "No. Are you crazy?" It is their way of protecting themselves from the possibility of being rejected, ridiculed, or treated as if they are crazy. Never settle for the first "no." Pursue it with words of understanding such as, "Look, with everything happening in your life (list the incidents) and with the way you have been feeling, it is normal to feel like ending it all. It's not crazy. So, have you thought about it?" This shows you are serious, care, understand, and are free to talk about it. If they have been thinking about it, they are likely to tell after this. If they are not suicidal, they will still respect the caring and concern and be more liable to come for help when in trouble.[6]

Here are some right things to say:
- "I didn't know how serious things had gotten. Let's talk about it.
- "It sounds like you are feeling totally hopeless. I understand how you can feel like ending it all. Have you told anyone else? We've got to talk to someone about this."
- "I don't want you to do anything to hurt yourself. I don't know how we can change the feeling, but I know there are people who can help."
- "I can't watch you twenty-four hours a day. If you want to, you'll find a way, but I don't want you to, and I will do anything to keep you from killing yourself."
- "I want to hear everything that's been happening. I've got the time." (Be sure you do, and be willing to drop everything if you don't.)

Now, it's important, too, to know what *not* to say. Here are a few statements to bear in mind:
- "You'll get over it. Things will be better tomorrow."

Things may not be better tomorrow, and making this kind of promise may make you part of the problem rather than the solution.

- "You have your whole life ahead of you."

    The suicidal person is usually convinced that that "whole life ahead" is bleak and not worth living.

- "You don't really feel that way."

    Yes, the suicidal person does feel that way.

- "You'd never really do it."

    How do you know? Over fifty thousand American teenagers have done it in just the past ten years.

So, the bottom line is: Don't criticize, judge, ridicule, minimize, or promise anything you can't deliver.

5. *Take action.* A suicidal threat is not like the alarm on your clock radio. You can't push a snooze button and wait a while longer before doing something. Immediate action is called for.

- Tell your friend about the sources of help.

    Find the number of your local suicide hotline (there probably is one). It's best that your friend make the decision to seek professional help, but be willing to make the arrangements and go along to lend your support.

- If a specific suicide plan has been revealed, be prepared to remove the instruments of the method if possible.

- Get your friend to make a binding agreement with you.

    Cynthia Taylor suggests: "Ask for a verbal contract with you that he or she will contact you or another designated person if he or she has thoughts of suicide."[7]

- Pray before, after, and during your encounter with a suicidal friend.

- If your friend refuses to get help, contact the

individual's parents or another responsible adult. Crisis intervention counselor Rose Wall says, "The person may say, 'Don't tell my parents,' but usually the person wants someone to know."[8] Even if you have made a promise of secrecy, break it for the sake of the person's life. Keeping a friend is more important than keeping your word in this case.

If you fail to act when a friend is in grave danger, and your friend succeeds at suicide, you will be haunted for years by the ghost of guilt. Don't let it happen.

Sometimes I'm overwhelmed by what teenagers tell me they're going through. They open up to me, I suppose, because in many cases I'm the first person they have heard address the problem plaguing their hearts. I tell teenagers everywhere, listen to your friends—some of them are in real danger and you don't know it. Let me wrap this up with a letter I received from Bridgette in Colorado:

> I have been really having a lot of problems. . . . Over the summer a lot of my friends who I looked up to turned to drugs and drinking. Right now I am caught in the middle of a lot of things. One girl tried to commit suicide and is now paralyzed. And another girl who I don't even know wants to melt my face in. She doesn't use her fists. She only uses guns and knives . . . but that doesn't bother me, well, not a lot. But I have been thinking about getting on drugs again. That really scares me, but I have really been thinking about it. . . .
>
> Well, right now I am really seriously thinking about suicide. I have cut my wrists a couple of times. But I never find enough courage to do a really good job. I often find myself thinking of other ways. But so far I haven't found a foolproof plan. Right now I don't think I have the courage. But with each passing day I get a little more. I see a real problem coming. I am reaching out to you. Please help.

18

Why *Not* Suicide?
An Open Letter from Jerry Johnston

Dear Teenage Friend:

In this book I've tried to share my truest, deepest feelings with you. I know it's a message that must be shared. A message of life. A message of hope. A message for you, because you matter.

Maybe you're one of the thousands of teenagers who have struggled with end-it-all thoughts. Perhaps you've even tried to take your life, but not succeeded. Thank God for that. And, of course, it's possible you have never thought about suicide at all. But at some point you may, and you need to be prepared to handle it.

The question around which I've built this book is, Why suicide? Everybody asks that in the aftermath of the tragedy. And as we've discovered, there are some evident, identifiable reasons and answers. But there is also another vital question I want you to think about: Why *not* suicide?

There are some really good reasons why you should not take your own life. For one, no suicide method is foolproof. Oh, you think you've got one that can't miss? Why don't you talk to the young man who put a gun under his chin, blew off practically his entire face, *and survived*. His girlfriend wrote to tell me the story. Hers is one of the most shocking letters I have ever received.

Suppose you do "succeed" in the attempt to end your life. Do you want to be guilty of murder also? How is that possible, you ask? Chances are, you will prompt somebody to think about committing suicide just because you have, and maybe, just maybe, that person will also "succeed." It has happened hundreds of times before. You have no guarantee of being an exception.

Suicide, when it works, is final. Maybe that sounds insultingly elementary. I mention it only because so many teenagers I've talked to have gotten the stupid idea that suicide is temporary, that somehow they're going to come back like the actor who dies in one movie and lives again in another. It doesn't work that way. Suicide is a permanent solution to temporary problems.

Like the parents of Aaron Stoufer said, the survivors are never the same. If you kill yourself, you will drastically change the lives of others who love you. You will ruin their lives, but you will be the biggest loser.

The saddest thing about suicide is that a person's potential is lost forever. And his or her purpose is snuffed out as crudely as a boot heel crushing a cigarette butt. Kill yourself, and you will stop dreams from coming true. Do you really want it that way?

Remember, my friend, your problems are temporary. They may seem now like a storm that will never pass, but the rains *will* stop, the sky *will* lighten, the clouds *will* drift away, and the sunshine *will* reappear. If you break up with somebody, you may feel that your whole world has caved in and that nothing will ever be the same. I remember those feelings very well, and the hurt does run deep. But it *does* go away, and it's sure not worth killing yourself over.

Don't ever make a big decision when you're under stress. That's like assuring that you'll make the wrong move. I doubt that anyone ever committed suicide when not under some kind of stress. Oh, the suicidal person may seem calm on the outside, but inside there are churning and boiling emotions.

Please, please, get rid of any glamorous idea you might have of suicide. If you take a bunch of pills, you won't just drift off into an eternal sleep. As you die, your sphincter muscles will relax, and your excrement will come out and make you an ugly sight indeed. If you shoot yourself, who is going to clean up the mess? Somebody has to do it.

There is hope. There are people who care. Turn to them in your time of greatest tension. Call the suicide hotline. Talk to someone you trust who can give wise counsel. If you feel that you don't have anyone else, write to me. I or one of my associates will help.

Why *not* suicide? *You* are the answer to that question. Your life is too valuable, too meaningful, too promising. Choose life.

Your friend,

Jerry Johnston

19

The Beginning

This may be the end of the book, but it's an appropriate place to talk about beginnings. For me, the most important beginning of all took place one night in a summer camp when I was a teenager. You may recall that I mentioned the experience in Chapter 2. Remember what I said about hearing a message that changed my life? Well, I'd like to share that message with you, because it led to the beginning of a new life for Jerry Johnston.

Bob Werner, the camp speaker, told in a firm but sensitive way about how God loves us and has a purpose for our lives. He talked about sin, about how it destroys God's purpose and leaves a person lonely and empty. I knew the cold, hard reality of that in my own heart. He went on to say that death is eventually going to claim every one of us. Then he concluded with a simple question that still rings in my memory. He asked, "If you were to die tonight, where would you go?"

When he mentioned death, my mind raced back

to that telephone call, the bottle of pills, the threats, the desire to kill myself. While all those thoughts were running wild, I heard Bob say, "The Bible says you can know that if you were to die tonight you would go to heaven." I wanted that kind of certainty.

He continued, "There is a heaven, and there is a hell. Your sin has separated you from God. In the state you are in you cannot have fellowship with God. But God cared for you so much that He allowed Jesus Christ His Son to die for your sins, in your place." Bob quoted from the Bible: "For the wages of sin is death, but the gift of God is eternal life in Christ Jesus our Lord." And he explained that when Jesus rose from the dead, He defeated death—for me. Jesus said, "I am come that you might have life, and have it more abundantly."

The message was getting through to me as he said, "If you want your sins forgiven, if you want peace and purpose in your life, if you want to go to heaven when you die, pray this simple prayer:

Dear God,
I know that I'm a sinner. I believe Jesus Christ died and rose from the dead for me. Right now, by faith, I invite Him to come into my life and save me. Thank You for the gift of eternal life. Thank You for the assurance that I am part of Your family and will go to heaven when I die.
In Jesus' Name, Amen.

With all the sincerity in me, I prayed that prayer that eventful night. Instantaneously, the peace of God flooded my being. I knew my life was changed! It was more than a good feeling, more than an emotional high. This was deep and certain. This was the new beginning I longed for. I wept with a gladness I'd never experienced.

From that point on, I have never regretted making that decision to put my full trust in Jesus Christ. And more than anything else, I desire to see others make that same decision.

Oh, yes, I've had lots of problems in the years since that night at camp. No life is without struggles and temptations. But none of the problems has been too great to overcome. I can say I've never had another suicidal thought. I know that in Jesus Christ I have perfect confidence. Because to receive Him is to receive life—true, spiritual life.

If you would like more information about experiencing this new beginning in your life, or if you have a question about anything presented in this book, feel free to contact me. My address is P.O. Box 12193, Overland Park, KS 66212. Telephone (913) 492-2066.

Remember: Choose Life.

Notes

Chapter 3

1. Centers for Disease Control, Department of Health and Human Services, *Morbidity and Mortality Weekly Report*, vol. 34, no. 24 (June 21, 1985), pp. 3–4.
2. Ibid.
3. Jeannye Thornton, "Behind a Surge in Suicides of Young People," *U. S. News & World Report* (June 20, 1983), p. 66.
4. "School Programs Fight Teen Suicide," *USA Today* (April 1, 1986), p. 1.
5. Carolyn H. Crowley and Richard Fitzbaugh, "To Die Will Be an Awfully Big Adventure," *US Magazine* (November 19, 1984), pp. 42, 43.
6. Thornton.

Chapter 4

1. "Having Babies," *Life* (March 1986), p. 33.
2. "School Contraceptives," *Kansas City Star* (October 10, 1985), p. 2A.

3. "The Games Teenagers Play," *Newsweek* (September 1, 1980), p. 49.
4. Claudia Wallis, "Children Having Children," *Time* (December 9, 1985), p. 82.
5. Special Report, *Alan Guttmacher Institute*, 1985.
6. *The Educational Forum*, vol. 50, no. 2 (Winter 1986).
7. Richard Stengel, "Children Having Children," *Time* (December 9, 1985), pp. 79, 80.
8. *Forum*.
9. Sally Helms and Robert Tenenbaum, "Kids and Sex," *Columbus Monthly* (November 1981), pp. 58–66.
10. Elizabeth Winship, "How to Talk with Teenagers," *Life* (March 1986), p. 69.
11. Patricia Bosworth, "Let's Call It Suicide," *Vanity Fair* (March 1985), p. 52.

Chapter 5

1. Pat Ordovensky and John DuBois, "Students: Alcohol is Enemy No. 1," *USA Today* (June 25, 1986), pp. 1–2D.

Chapter 6

1. Peggy Mann, *Marijuana Alert* (New York: McGraw-Hill, 1985), pp. 18–19.
2. *Weekly Reader* (January 7–21, 1986), p. 1.
3. John DuBois, "Teens Say Buying Drugs 'A Piece of Cake,'" *USA Today* (July 28, 1986), p. 1.
4. Mann.
5. John S. Long and Ronald A. Taylor, "America on Drugs," *U.S. News & World Report* (July 28, 1986), pp. 48, 49.
6. Vern E. Smith, "A World Called Desire," *Newsweek* (June 2, 1986), p. 23.
7. Long and Taylor.
8. Bob Meehan with Stephen J. Meyer, "Is Your Child Taking Drugs?" *Reader's Digest* (July 1986), p. 57.
9. Todd Brewster, "What's In, What's Out," *Life* (March 1986), p. 46.
10. "Kids and Cocaine," *Newsweek* (March 17, 1986), p. 58.

11. Jack McCallum, "Death of a Dream," *Sports Illustrated* (June 30, 1986), p. 27.
12. Long and Taylor.
13. Jacob V. Lamar, "Crack," *Time* (June 2, 1986), p. 16.
14. Marjory Roberts, "Drug Abuse," *Psychology Today* (June 1986), p. 14.
15. Mann, pp. 239–40.
16. Diana Maycheck, "Bret Ellis Is Too Hip for Hype," *Mademoiselle* (June 1986), p. 66.
17. Ibid.

Chapter 7

1. Flora Davis, "The MTV VJs: Airheads of the Air," *Mademoiselle* (January 1986), p. 58.
2. Ibid.
3. Ibid.
4. 1985 Yearbook, *Rolling Stone* (December 1985), p. 53.
5. Roger Wolmuth, "Parents vs. Rock," *People* (September 16, 1985), p. 49.
6. Sylvie Simmons, "Ozzy Drops the Bomb," *Creem* (July 1986), p. 10.
7. Ibid., pp. 10–11.
8. News item, "Rockers' Rights," *Picture Week* (August 25, 1986), p. 73.
9. 1985 Yearbook, p. 89.
10. "Madonna, Like Marilyn, Likes It Hot," *USA Today* (August 29, 1986). p. 2D.
11. 1985 Yearbook, p. 89.
12. Merle Ginsberg, *Boy George* (New York: Dell, 1984). p. 19.
13. Joe Dietrich, *Boy George and Culture Club* (New York: Cherry Lane Books, 1984), p. 28.
14. Kevin J. Koffler and Rick Sky, "The Tears of a Clown," *Spin Magazine* (October 1986), p. 92.
15. Bill Baro with Barbara Rosen, "I Am a Heroin Junkie," *Newsweek* (July 21, 1986), p. 55.
16. Carol Leggett, *The Heavy Metal Bible* (New York: Pinnacle, 1985), pp. 4–5.
17. Sue Cummings, "Asleep at the Wheel," *Spin* (January 1986), pp. 72, 81.
18. Leggett, p. 53.
19. Ibid., p. 54.

20. Diana Washington, "Fad or Fanatic Cult? El Paso Teenagers Lured Into Devil Worship," *El Paso Times* (February 16, 1986), p. 1.
21. Ibid.
22. Leggett, p. 99.

Chapter 8

1. John Weldon and James Bjornstad, *Playing with Fire* (Chicago: Moody, 1984), p. 18.
2. Geoffrey Smith, "Dungeons and Dragons," *Forbes* (September 15, 1980), p. 139.
3. Phyllis Ten Elshof, "Dungeons and Dragons: A Fantasy Fad or Dabbling in the Demonic?" *Christianity Today* (September 4, 1981), p. 56.
4. John Eric Holmes, "Confessions of a Dungeon Master," *Psychology Today* (November 1980), p. 84.
5. Elshof, p. 56.
6. Weldon and Bjornstad, p. 19.
7. Ibid., p. 20.
8. News item, *Christianity Today* (May 17, 1985), p. 64.
9. Ibid.

Chapter 9

1. Television program, "Nightline," ABC Network (November 1984).
2. Steven Stack, "A Leveling Off in Young Suicide," *The Wall Street Journal* (Wednesday, May 28, 1986), p. 34.
3. George Howard Colt, "The Enigma of Suicide," *Harvard Magazine* (September–October 1983), pp. 47–48.
4. "Nightline."
5. Rhea Zakich, "Secrets of Family Communications," *Reader's Digest* (August 1986), p. 160.

Chapter 10

1. "When Hopelessness Sets In, Warns Psychiatrist Aaron Beck, Suicide Can Be Close Behind," *People* (April 7, 1986), p. 93.
2. Ibid., pp. 93–94.

Chapter 12

1. "Tragedy Mars Abuse Speech," The *Oregon City Enterprise-Courier*, Gladstone, Oregon (May 3, 1985), p. 1.

Chapter 13

1. Marcia Seligson, "Are You Suicidal?" *Harper's Bazaar* (August 1972), pp. 62–63.
2. Ibid., p. 63.
3. Ibid.
4. N. L. Farberow, *Some Facts About Suicide* (Washington, D.C.: U.S. Government Printing Office, 1961), p. 12.
5. Seligson, p. 62.

Chapter 14

1. "Heed Warning Signs If Teen Seems Suicidal" *Kansas City Times* (March 22, 1984), pp. B3–4.
2. George Howe Colt, "The Painful Riddle of Teen Suicide," *Seventeen* (April 1985), pp. 184–87.
3. Tim LaHaye, *How to Win Over Depression* (Grand Rapids, Mich.: Zondervan, 1979), p. 24.

Chapter 16

1. Pamela Cantor, "Schools Must Help These Tragedies," *USA Today* (February 26, 1986).

Chapter 17

1. Cynthia Taylor, "Helping the Suicidal," *Eternity* (March 1985), p. 32.
2. Ibid.
3. Robert J. Barry, "Teenage Suicide: An American Tragedy," *FBI Law Enforcement Bulletin* (April 1986), p. 17.
4. "But for the grace of God . . . ," *U.S. News & World Report* (February 24, 1986), p. 5.
5. William Steele, "Preventing the Spread of Suicide Among Adolescents," *USA Today Magazine* (November 1985), p. 59.
6. Ibid.
7. Taylor, p. 32.
8. Aurora Mackey, "The Frightening Facts About Teen Suicide," *Teen Magazine* (October 1983), p. 94.

For Further Help

Youth. 800-554-KIDS.

LifeLine, Jerry Johnston Association, P.O. Box 12193, Overland Park, KS 66212. 913-492-2066.

Suicide Hotline. Consult your local phone directory or call directory assistance. Such hotlines have different names from city to city, so check for "Crisis Intervention Services." Of course, you can also contact the local mental health association.

PRIDE (Parent Resource Institute for Drug Education). 800-241-7946.

National Federation of Parents for Drug-Free Youth. 800-554-KIDS.

American Council for Drug Education. 301-984-5700.

Life Exposé with Jerry Johnston

VHS or BETA Video Format
(Running Time: 46 minutes)
Also available on 16mm and Audio Cassette

The *Life Exposé* is Jerry Johnston's nationally acclaimed message on teen suicide and drug abuse. This powerful video presentation features Jerry live speaking to over 2,000 students with the message that has created great impact in the lives of young people. Sixteen teenagers briefly share their personal stories of suicide attempts or contemplation which are integrated at key points in the lecture. There is instant rapport created with the listener as this video details the reasons and peer-to-peer warning signs of a suicidal. The conclusion leaves an impression never-to-be-forgotten as Jerry plays an actual recorded message of a teenager talking to his mother immediately prior to killing himself. The words are typed on the screen for the listener to follow and understand the damaging steps to self-destruction. This is a video that will not be forgotten, and it is excellent for teenagers, parents, classroom settings, and for counseling purposes.

The Cure to Suicide and Suicidal Thinking

by Jerry Johnston

This informative booklet gives solid answers to the person whose friend or relative may have committed suicide as well as to the person who may be considering taking his or her own life. A step-by-step procedure for gaining victory over depressive thoughts is outlined, and Jerry shares the positive steps he himself took to change the direction of his life. This attractive booklet is a must for the person who wants to rise above suicidal thinking and not return to that mode of thought. One copy is available free to each respondent. If more than one copy is needed, quantity orders can be filled at minimal cost.

For more information on these products, write to:
Jerry Johnston Association
P.O. Box 12193
Overland Park, KS 66212